C000070154

LIFE BEYOND DEATH

SARUM THEOLOGICAL LECTURES

LIFE BEYOND DEATH

Threads of Hope in Faith, Life and Theology

Vernon White

DARTON · LONGMAN + TODD

First published in 2006 by
Darton, Longman and Todd Ltd
1 Spencer Court
140–142 Wandsworth High Street
London SW18 4JJ

© 2006 Vernon White

The right of Vernon White to be identified as the author of this work has been
asserted in accordance with the Copyright, Designs and Patents Act 1998.

ISBN-10: 0-232-52686-9
ISBN-13: 978-0-232-52686-8

A catalogue record for this book is available from the British Library.

Typeset by YHT Ltd, London
Printed and bound in Great Britain by
The Cromwell Press, Trowbridge, Wiltshire

CONTENTS

PREFACE

This book has a clear readership in view, typified by those who attended the public lectures on which it is based. It is intended for thoughtful people who are familiar with Christian faith and doctrine, but who want to probe more deeply in the theological tradition. It is for those who want to face up constructively to the difficult issues that core beliefs of traditional faith now present to us. Its readership will include some who have academic theological training, and some who do not; lay Christians and ordained ministers; those whose main concern is to explore their own belief, and those who want to understand how others believe. It will include those who have a settled faith, and those who have major doubts. I hope that there is something here for all these, and perhaps others too.

Public lectures are a good forum for such a mix, and I am grateful to Sarum College and Salisbury Cathedral for providing the opportunity – and challenge – of preparing and delivering them with this in mind. A particular debt of gratitude is due to Professor David Catchpole for the tireless organisation and inspiration he devotes to every series of Sarum Lectures. I am also grateful to the publishers for their guidance, not least in encouraging me to offer a text very close to the original lectures themselves. Because a lecture is an *event*, its text never seems quite adequate to print as it stands, and there has been some adaptation. Nonetheless, the central four chapters remain as faithful as possible to the original lectures, and the last chapter gives at least a taste of the actual conversation of questions and answers which followed each one.

The choice of subject matter – life beyond death – was wholly mine. Whether this subject proves to be as useful and important as I believe, now needs to be judged by others, as they read what follows.

INTRODUCTION

Life after death, like religion itself, will not go away. The death of afterlife is often confidently announced, along with the death of God, but it refuses to lie down and die. Instead it is the death of death which continues to fascinate the world and haunt our hopes. Rumours of heaven remain in post-modernity as much as pre-modernity – and they are part of young people's thinking as much as for older people.

Admittedly, some reasons for this continuing belief are not persuasive. The fact that speculation about it can flourish in our current pluralist mindset might make us more suspicious of it, rather than less. In a spiritual smorgasbord where anything goes, the mere existence of a particular belief is unremarkable. It has no special claim to being true just by being believed. And in any case, this particular belief is always likely to survive because it so readily lends itself to wish fulfilment, so it is not surprising that it can arise in almost any social or intellectual context.

For all that, the belief and hope in an afterlife is still there, and has to be reckoned with. It will not do to regard it simply as a function of a particularly credulous culture, or individual wishful thinking. In fact, the opposite is sometimes the case. A radical, full-blown belief in the survival (or re-creation) of personal consciousness is not as easy as it may seem. Sometimes it has had to fight its way *into* social and individual credibility, rather than naturally arising out of it. Even within major religious traditions its role cannot be assumed. So we cannot dismiss it just as an inevitable by-product of our desires.

For the same reason, even when it has been clearly and consistently maintained in a religious tradition (like Christianity), it cannot be taken for granted and must not be neglected. Yet it has been, and this creates the conundrum which has helped galvanise this short book. The belief has faltered in current Christian proclamation (where we might expect it to be most supported), even though it often persists in some form outside the church (where it might seem less supported). The hope is diminishing in church and in theology, even though we still encounter it in popular speculation. We hear it proclaimed less confidently and less frequently within the very faith which has been so significant in helping to give birth to it and nurture it.

Why is this? The question wouldn't be worth pursuing if the belief was reckoned to be marginal to Christian faith. Yet I have a hunch that it is actually pivotal to both faith and theology. I believe it is integral to the continued credibility of theism itself – something I shall argue later. Moreover, because it is a belief about life-giving *hope*, it will connect with some of the deepest hopes of the world at large, and so the urgency of proclaiming it confidently is even greater. For all these reasons it must be put back higher on the agenda of the Gospel, and that is the main purpose of this short book. I simply want to help restore credibility and confidence in believing this hope, and believing that it matters.

Because it is such a short book, however, I must acknowledge its limits – and its assumptions. For a start, I am largely assuming that Christian faith is intrinsically *theistic*. That is, I assume Christian faith has God at its heart, and I assume that the meaning of God is personal. I take it that a theistic 'God' includes the sense of an objective, personal, relational, agent who transcends us, as well as being bound up with us. To be sure, such words as 'transcendent', 'personal', 'relational', 'agent' have to be stretched in their usual meanings when they are used of God. That is an inevitable consequence of the mystery of God. Nonetheless, they cannot be entirely abandoned, for in the end the irreducible meaning of theism is that when we meet 'God' in Christian faith it means meeting *something like another personal reality*. Put another way, God is not just a name either for an impersonal force, or for the projection of our subjective feelings and aspirations.

This may not seem a contentious starting point for most Christian believers. But it still needs to be made clear at a time when popular spirituality is reshaping the language of traditional religion to give it quite different meanings – and when even some Christian theology wishes to do the same.[1] The assumption of a theistic religion increasingly has to defend itself, not just for its intellectual coherence but also for its moral and social standing. As critics are quick to point out, God as a transcendent, powerful, personal 'other' can provoke fear and loathing as well as incredulity. Even as I write this, C. S. Lewis's Lion – an imaginative outworking of his robust theism – is bounding beguilingly onto the big screen, but he is by no means universally liked, let alone believed.[2] In fact I believe that confident theism, properly understood, is a liberating belief, not an oppressive one – and Christian faith will not be thanked in the long-term for abandoning it or letting it die by a thousand qualifications. However, I do need to make clear that this book does not argue this case: it largely assumes it.

A second assumption is the existence and significance of the personal self. I assume that we are people with a unique personal, relational, and valuable identity. We have sufficient enduring 'substance' to our identity for our personal stories through time and history to *matter*, to have significance. 'You' and 'I' (and especially you and I together) are not simply a fleeting set of unrelated experiences or impressions, nor are we just a temporary social construction. We are uniquely and irreducibly *ourselves*. Again, this is not obviously a controversial belief amongst most Christian believers. It is also still a widespread common assumption beyond the bounds of faith. But again it needs to be recognized as an assumption – especially at a time when some popular and philosophical preoccupations with the self have become very sceptical of this view of selfhood.[3]

These two assumptions are very closely linked. They are certainly interdependent in Christian theology, as I have discussed elsewhere.[4] They are also so pivotal to the particular matter in hand – life after death – that we shall never leave them behind entirely as we launch into it. They will keep surfacing in what follows, and they will help sustain it. And at least this will show how the overall argument has a coherence and inter-connectedness about it, even though some of its assumptions have not been fully argued. For there is strength in such coherence, even in this strange kaleidoscope of late modernity where fragments of belief seem to stand quite alone and overall patterns or systems are viewed with suspicion. After all, sus-tainable and credible beliefs are unlikely to be wholly unrelated!

Another major limit to this discussion will be its concentration on the Christian form of the belief, rather than its form in other religions. This is not, I hasten to say, because I want to imply that other religions have no light to shed. It is because I want to avoid the presumption of speaking for other traditions when I cannot know them all adequately. I believe it shows more respect to be reticent about them, than to speak misleadingly about them. Another reason is the one I have signalled already: I believe the Christian form of the belief has itself become neglected – it needs revisiting and putting on the agenda. To bring it into closer dialogue with the insights of other religions might well help in this task, but I have not attempted it here, and that is a limitation.

Of course, even within these limits it could still be thought much too ambitious. The subject matter is the problem, for how can we talk sensibly of life beyond death at all? Because thought and language is bound by the limits of our finitude, isn't life beyond death inevitably out of bounds for *any* serious discussion? We cannot speak anything about what we have not experienced – so should we not be silent? As the philosopher Wittgenstein famously remarked, 'whereof one cannot speak, thereof one must be silent'.

Perhaps. But not entirely – provided we also admit some other limits. For instance, to begin with I shall not try to say much about the *nature* of life beyond death – what it might be like. My main concern is to explore the significance of the bare belief that there is something beyond death, not to speculate too much on what it's like. I want to put some hint of heaven on the map, but

I'm not offering a detailed travel guide to what heaven might be like. Admittedly it will be hard to remain within these limits. It is impossible to talk about a belief's significance without *any* sense at all of what it is we're talking about: like trying to imagine fine wine when we have never even tasted tea; like trying to talk about love when we have never even met anyone at all. Nonetheless, overall I will concentrate much more on the 'that' of life beyond death, rather than the 'what'.

Yet because at least some sense of 'what' we may expect is unavoidable there is this other major assumption which I readily make. In the end I assume that it *is* possible to think and imagine beyond ourselves, *in some measure*, and whatever the difficulties. There are, after all, powerful theological warrants for this. The doctrine of creation provides them. The moment we think at all of God beyond us as Creator we must expect some imprint of that beyondness will be accessible to us in his creation (and in us). As Augustine said, eternity will inevitably be 'set in the heart of man'. There are also theological warrants in the doctrines of revelation and redemption. The transcendent God leaves His[5] mark not just generally in created structures, but also in specific, saving, events. Some aroma of eternity must therefore be found in those particular events, and we should expect that some particular events of history and experience will specially connect us to that 'beyondness in things'. From the burning bush to the cross and resurrection of Christ there have been such extraordinary, 'godful', events. These have stretched and transformed the normal fabric of life so that they have let in cracks of eternity (and thereby helped us to see those cracks in ordinary life as well). And from these signs of eternity within ourselves, and our world, we shall therefore be able to speak something of eternity beyond.

There are also philosophical warrants for this assumption: i.e. for our capacity to think beyond direct experience. These appear chiefly in idealist philosophy, though I cannot pursue that here. There are even some kinds of warrants in recent science. In its references to quantum fields and subatomic realities, science is now attempting to talk of invisible realities beyond direct experience. It thinks it can do so because these other realities beyond experience leave a sort of trail of effects within our experience. This is at least an analogy of the 'trail of the holy' in this world. It mirrors the way that glimpses of God's transcendence and eternity are picked up in their effects, even if not directly perceived.

These encouragements to speak of the beyond still require us to be cautious. They always require us to stretch the language and thought we use. They need us to remember that we shall almost always be using language symbolically, using words which express both a likeness and unlikeness with their usual meaning. This is something that poets have always appreciated – and something that theology, at its best, has always taken on board. So when we say, for example, 'I believe in the resurrection of the body' we do not mean it woodenly and literally as if some exact resemblance of our present material bodies is brought back out of the grave. It will be no more like that, surely, than Robert Burns' love which is 'like a red, red rose' will be literally like a fragrant, prickly plant! Instead we will mean a radically new way of being ourselves, which extends the normal use of language.

Yet, for all this proper caution, there are these warrants for at least trying to think and articulate the beyond. Again, I have not argued them. They operate largely as assumptions, but they do at least license the way the discussion can now unfold.

It does so like this. Chapter one will set the scene: first by a brief review of the current status of the belief in contemporary church and wider society; second, by trawling ordinary experience to look for signs of its persistence – those so-called 'signs of transcendence' which are embedded in the deep structure of general experience. In the second chapter I will begin the exploration of the belief in the Judaeo-Christian faith tradition, especially the western theological tradition. In the third chapter I look more specifically at Christian beliefs about resurrection – what they imply about the relation between time and eternity, body and soul, the individual and the cosmos as a whole. In the final chapter I consider issues of truth and morality: the way belief in afterlife shapes and guides the way we live here and now. The postscript will pick up some of the questions all this provoked when it was presented as a series of lectures.

No doubt it will also raise other questions which remain unanswered. But if it at least helps put the subject back into serious contention I will be pleased. And if it actually helps strengthen hope and belief, then I shall be delighted.

Chapter 1

THE PERSISTENCE OF
TRANSCENDENCE

I have claimed it is at least possible to talk about this subject, if only speculatively, but that raises another preliminary question to pursue. Even if it is possible, why is it important? Why does it matter to put heaven on the map?

One answer was given almost exactly 40 years ago in a series of lectures called the 'Holland' lectures (named after Henry Scott Holland, author of the famous – or infamous – phrase 'death is nothing at all'). In fact the lecturer himself was not Holland but the former Archbishop Michael Ramsey – and the book which emerged from the lectures anything but infamous.[1] It is a remarkable book: deceptively simple, characteristically lucid, and profound. In it he gives this answer to why heaven matters, at least for the Christian believer. He believes that essential Christian faith is, inseparably, *both* this-worldly *and* otherworldly. He argues that whenever scripture and doctrine are most illuminating about this world, it is always by reference to the otherworld. He admits that the language which has to be used to express the otherworldly dimension is difficult to express credibly and needs to be expressed symbolically. But he insists this can and must still be done – precisely because we cannot simply strip out the otherworldly dimension and leave anything recognizably Christian in our attitude to this world. That is why we must keep struggling with the language of eternity.

He gives three examples of this: i.e. examples of essential Christian attitudes to this world which spring directly from keeping our nerve about the otherworldly dimension. First, the reality of eternity means our reverence for other persons is deepened; second, authentic humility is encouraged; and third, creative fortitude in the face of suffering is made more possible. He further suggests that eternity may be necessary for the very nature of God to be credible. I will return to all these points later – in fact much of what will follow will be a sort of unfolding of these basic ideas of Ramsey's. But for now they can simply serve as headlines about why this belief matters. For Ramsey all this is at stake, and that is why we must not lose our nerve about making the case for eternity.

Of course, even if we agree it matters, we might still want to ask whether there is still any need to argue the case. After all, Ramsey was writing back in the 1960s – at a time when (I quote) 'modern man capitulated easily to hard-nosed rational secularism and reductionism'. In other words it was an intellectual climate when the otherworldly beliefs of Christian faith were particularly under threat – but as I have already hinted in the introduction, that climate may now have changed 40 years on. We are now generally more hospitable to spirituality and mystery – and those severe prophets of secularism of the 1960s and 70s who predicted an inexorable secularisation have had to backtrack. We now live with the more fluid, playful sensibilities of post-modern man and woman, less persuaded by rationalism or secularism, more able to entertain a variety of spiritual beliefs, from astrology to reincarnation. Institutional religion may still be declining, but this general spirituality has not. So perhaps this is no longer a battle to be fought? Maybe life after death is no longer a difficult, declining, unfashionable notion?

The picture is not that straightforward, however. Although there is this plethora of new beliefs, the element of hard-nosed rationalism has not gone away. It is still a major player – and if anything it is being reinvigorated as a counter to some of the excesses of the new spiritual climate. The irrational nature of current laissez-faire spiritual consumerism (and the different kind of irrationalism of fundamentalism) is actually provoking a renewed rationally-based scepticism about *all* religious belief. In any case, even within the more fluid world of many spiritual beliefs, the form they take is often very shapeless and shifting. They may well include speculation about some form of ongoing life, but do not necessarily include specific, ethically-based belief in *personal* life after death of the sort I want to deal with: i.e. they don't necessarily encourage the notion of the personal self beyond death, granted by a personal creator God. That sort of belief, recent evidence shows, is still rare – and so Ramsey's concern is still justified. Nerve has been lost – especially within the churches. Many within church do not believe in it much now, whatever the mixed picture outside the church.

Some of the evidence for this comes from a sociological survey carried out in the mid 1990s by Douglas Davies.[2] It showed that up to a third of Anglicans and a similar number of Methodists said they believed personal life simply came to an end at death, and only a third professed specific belief in a definite spiritual survival. Only four per cent believed in a resurrection of the whole person. The report comments dryly: 'Given that [resurrection] lies at the heart of [Christian] worship and theology...one might, perhaps, have expected to see the idea of the resurrection being chosen more often by more of the churches' members'. One might indeed! We should note that it is a patchy picture, and a more recent survey of churchgoers in a specific context showed rather more belief.[3] Nonetheless, Davies has maintained that there is nothing to suggest anything different from his earlier findings in overall trends.

If the belief in afterlife is at least insecure, and possibly fading, why is this? There are a number of reasons. As I have said, there is still the persistence of straightforward rational secularism: there is the ready recourse to rational and natural explanations for what had previously been thought to be supernatural. What we used to think lies beyond this life is easily seen simply as projection and illusion, wishful thinking fed by our psychological or biological needs. That has been the main storyline of Feuerbach and Freud, Durkheim and Dawkins, and it remains highly influential. For others there are also political and moral concerns. The afterlife is suspect because its hopes and rewards can be used manipulatively by the powerful to keep the poor content with their this worldly lot and de-motivate them from improving that lot. That was the Marxist storyline, and that too hasn't gone away. There have also been important social reasons. Because of changes in society we have become distanced from death. The medicalizing of death and dying in hospitals, and the rationalized disposal of bodies in crematoria and mass municipal graves because of population growth, has meant we are only rarely in touch with people dying in our homes. Only rarely do we bury our own dead, only rarely do we walk though churchyards amongst our own departed. All this has the overall effect of removing the mystery of death and mortality from our midst, replacing it with an impersonal and industrialized process – thereby suppressing any thoughts of what might lie beyond death. There are signs that this too may now be changing, and death is being 'reintroduced' to us. But the overall pull is still in the opposite direction, especially because it has also been reinforced by more subtle social changes in our experience and conception of *time*. Because of our culture of consumerism and its offer of instant gratification, the experience of linear time (i.e. having to *wait* for one thing to follow another) is fading – the present is all. So any sense of a beyond, any sense of 'after', fades with it.

Such social changes, according to sociologist Tony Walter, may be even more significant than the continued pressures of rationalism, and they certainly act cumulatively with it.[4] They also act cumulatively with Christianity's overall decline as a whole world-view in which belief in an afterlife has been too often packaged with discredited and incredible images of life beyond death – bizarre second comings of Christ, lurid details of heaven and hell. As such, it has been hard to retain belief in afterlife itself, apart from those wider images. All these are reasons why the belief has declined.

Later I will explore some ripostes to these challenges. For example, the last point about the difficulties generated by traditional imagery returns us to the need not to take language too woodenly. The moral point about social abuse of the belief needs to be countered by pointing to the positive fruits of it, such as Ramsey's trio of reverence, hope, humility. The pressures from rationalism can be dealt with in their own terms, not just by questioning the sovereignty of reason. I will return to all these points. But for now I simply want to underline the force of these challenges themselves, in order to set the scene as honestly as I can: that is, to acknowledge a situation where, for all these reasons, specific notions of transcendence, and life beyond death, still face a cold climate. It is a climate which *has* caused us to lose our nerve within Church life, and that is why it is important to re-establish some confidence in it and make a case for it.

So now to making that case itself. And to begin I want first to sketch out positive signs of transcendence in our general, shared, human experience. In other words, I will scan some of the signs which, in traditional theological terms, we pick up because of 'general revelation', because nature is itself 'graced'. This will then set a scene in which the more specific theological beliefs of faith and revelation can be better considered in due course.

But what does it mean to look for signs of transcendence in 'general experience'? I do not mean we can expect *all* experience to yield such signs. To talk about general experience does not necessarily mean universal experience. As post-modernists insist, we are likely to be claiming too much if we claim any experience is true for everyone at any time and any place. So I am simply seeking signs in what many may recognize as ordinary experience, not what all must recognize. Likewise, I do not mean that our general experience is nothing but signs of the transcendent. The world is not so 'charged with the grandeur of God' (Hopkins) that eternity flows effortlessly and seamlessly through our experience and we just can't miss it. As Catholic theologian Balthasar puts it, we cannot 'smooth out the drama, difficulty, and finitude of experience' like that. For although nature may indeed be graced, it must also include 'space': there has to be space between infinite creator and finite creation. This is a positive space for freedom, but it will also distance us and obscure the divine signs and sounds. And this means that general experience presents us not just with grace and signs of presence: it also presents us with the absence of God – sometimes vast tracts of, gaping, aching, silence. It also means that if we *do* pick up signs they will be ambivalent, not decisive arguments. Moreover, even if we do find such signs they must not be mistaken for salvation itself. To reduce the meaning of salvation to picking up signs trivializes it to the level of those computer games where the player proceeds though a labyrinth by picking up little dollops of power to help him on his quest! In short – although we may appeal to general experience for signs, we must also accept their limitations. They will be neither universal, nor compelling, nor saving.

Nonetheless, I am convinced that there *are* such signs, and they are worth looking out for. There are 'intimations of immortality', if you like Wordsworth's phrase; 'immortal longings', if you prefer Shakespeare's; and they run as a golden thread through ordinary, general, human experience. So – where should we look first to find them?

One obvious place to begin might be the experience of death itself. After all, if we are looking for what might lie beyond a threshold, why not look most closely at the threshold? And I will certainly come to this. However, I do not want to begin there. For example, in my own experience death has *not*, so far, proved to be a particularly eloquent sign of transcendence. The force of my first personal brushes with death when travelling in Africa in younger days was neither to frighten me nor to offer me signs of the beyond. Instead, the experiences merely raised the stakes of life and energized me for more adventure. The insouciance of youth, no doubt! But, even later, as a parish priest, when I frequently encountered the death and dying of others, the effect was similar. Although I often found myself thinking, speaking, and listening with others about life after death, this was not always the immediate and instinctive outcome of the experience itself. The more usual outcome was actually to think less about what might happen next to the deceased and more about the meaning of the life they had just lived. More recently when my encounter with death has become much closer through personal bereavements, it has more sharply touched the raw nerve of my *own* mortality, but even then I have not found a sense of afterlife any more compelling. If anything the afterlife has sometimes seemed less clear and certain. I do not mention my experience to present it as normative, nor to explore the psychology of grief and loss. I mention it simply to illustrate in general this fact that death itself may not necessarily be the best or only place to look for clear signs of transcendence.

This is an important point to make particularly to help deflect some anthropological theories which have assumed too readily that we *only* arrive at our beliefs about God and the beyond from our encounter with death. Such theories about the inter-dependence of death and religious belief are pervasive. Starkly put, they simply suggest that death leads us to *invent* the hope of afterlife – and the very idea of God Himself – to give us solace in the face of our mortality. The anthropologist Malinowski, writing at the turn of the last century, was celebrated for this sort of view.[5] But my point is that this doesn't work. The connection between death and religious belief in afterlife is nothing like as clear as Malinowski wants it to be. My own experience is one small pointer to this, but there is also more substantial evidence to support it. For example, the very elderly – in clear proximity to death – generally show no signs of being more inclined to believe in life after death than others. If anything they are more ready to accept their finitude.[6] There are also much wider grounds for questioning the connection. For instance, it is a simple matter of fact that many religions exist which do not even include the promise of afterlife at all – so they at least could hardly have arisen out of fear of death (a point made forcefully by John Bowker).[7] In any case, truth isn't determined solely by determining the psychological or social origin of a belief. Even if a belief does take wing in the context of some mortal fear or mortal longing, that of itself does not mean the belief is necessarily wrong. My fear of death and ache for immortality does not mean there is no such thing as afterlife, any more than a fear of hunger and an ache for food means there is no such thing as food – a point I shall return to in chapter four.

So we should not assume death is the main focus of signs of eternity. Instead we might do better by looking first more closely at *life* and one person who has done this, in a way I have not found surpassed, is sociologist Peter Berger. He describes exactly what we are looking for: what he calls 'signals of transcendence' from ordinary human experience. These are signs found within our 'natural' reality which appear to point beyond that reality. They are not deeply buried symbols which have to be excavated from the unconscious (as with Jung's archetypes), but accessible signs which 'belong to ordinary everyday awareness'[8].

Here are two examples from amongst those he mentions. One is our sense of what he calls 'order'. This is the sense that ultimate reality is somehow 'all right', good, rational, purposeful. Although our current experience may well *not* be all right, and although we may have no evident reason to think ultimate reality will be, nonetheless the sense of final good order persists. It is a sort of faith people live by, whether or not they are conventionally religious or consciously subscribe to it. It is powerful and pervasive, more like an instinct than a belief – which is why it survives even against all evidence, even when it appears to be palpable nonsense.

Berger points for example to the familiar situation of a child beset in the night with nameless threats and fears, calling out for its mother. What is the mother's instinctive response? She will take the child in her arms and say, in a thousand different languages and in a thousand different ways: 'don't be afraid – *everything is all right*'. What is she doing? Just reassuring the child? Of course, but is that all? She knows she has no power to make everything all right – not *everything*. No parent can, much as we long to. So is she just hoping? Perhaps. But more than this, she is revealing this profound instinct about an ultimate good order. She is expressing the instinct that all will be well, thereby appealing to something which would have to be grounded in a reality beyond our mortal experience. She displays this not by any conscious rational belief but by her instinctual behaviour which is itself, therefore, a signal of transcendence – a pointer to something beyond.

Another of Berger's signals is the sense of play – joyful play, as known mostly by children. For play involves the suspension of normal time. A game creates its own time, different from the rules of time by which the rest of the natural or social world is bound (as exasperated parents know well!). Most normal adult living is linear: it is an inexorable march towards the next thing and ultimately – as Heidegger puts it – a 'living-unto-death'. But joyful play suspends this process, and in this way the play of children points to what Berger calls the 'deathlessness of child-hood'. As such it is also pointing to the deathlessness of us all, for even adults can sometimes play. In some poignant moments adults have played literally in the face of death: for example, in the fabled Christmas Day football match in the first world war trenches; or in the music of the Vienna Philharmonic as Soviet troops were entering the city; and did the band really play as the Titanic went down? Such playful behaviour is transcending normal time, so it is another instinctual sign of transcendence. And it is especially so when this play happens in the midst of young life, because that is when we see so clearly an immortal longing which is created not by imminent death but out of a celebration of life itself.

There are other such signals too: humour, for example. The sense of incongruity in this life which lies at the heart of humour is the hint that things in this life actually *do not fit,* they do not entirely add up. Humour sees this, and so hints implicitly at a beyond where the fit *is* possible. There is also the general experience of hope itself, which is so astonishingly resilient throughout the whole of life. Or there is the experience of journeying and never quite arriving, or story-telling without ever quite reaching a satisfactory end. This feeling that we are in an unresolved story or journey is a widely and deeply held experi-ence. It is an instinct of some sort of destiny which keeps pulling us forward even when we never see its end in this life. All these, and others, are signs and pointers to a fulfilment beyond what this world affords. Even the atheist Nietzsche acknowledged them, almost against his will. He sensed it, for example, in the very notion of truth and its transcendent claim on us, or in the experience of sheer delight: 'truth is divine', and 'all delight desires eternity', he said.

Turn from philosophers and sociologists to poets and we shall find yet more signs. To be sure, these will be shaped by a particular culture, yet they are still able to resonate widely. For example, from our own western tradition there is the recurring motif of *longing*. There is inconsolable longing which is an unfulfilled desire for something we do not quite know: as Thomas Traherne put it, it is an experience of 'a world of love to somewhat, but we know not what...' In the romantics like Wordsworth this longing sometimes seems to be identified with memory, moments in his past: they are 'intimations of immortality from recollections of early childhood'. At other times Wordsworth associated it with beauty, something which dwells in 'the mind of man and the light of setting suns'. In fact the key characteristic is that the longing does not settle exactly in any of these experiences, memory or beauty, past or present, for it remains precisely a longing. That is the whole point. Because it points from within experience to something beyond experience, it remains longing. That is why the more astringent later romantics and post-romantics will also express similar longing in the absence or silence of things. Thus we find Thomas Hardy in one poem looking at a young girl dancing through the empty spectacles of an old man. It is an image of longing for something which is not actually seen at all – yet because the longing is there, and we cannot long for something entirely unreal and unknown, it remains a hint of something. They are longings for what we don't know or see, yet still seem to half know.

In other words, all these poets are trying to express a texture to life which simply will not be resolved within this life. For they sense that even if we do get what we think we want to satisfy the longing in this life, the longing will remain. Even if we do gain access to good memories, natural beauties and reciprocal love, the ache remains. Even when we have access to good homes, we remain homesick. Something always remains unfulfilled because in this life we still do not fully *inhabit* these good experiences in a way which settles it. We remain slightly outside our experiences of what we love and desire, never wholly within. It is a bitter-sweet experience – and it is out of that bitter-sweetness that we realize it is a sign of something truly beyond. 'In speaking of this desire for our own far-off country', wrote C. S. Lewis, 'I am trying to rip open the inconsolable secret in each one of you – the secret which hurts so much that you take your revenge on it by calling it names like Nostalgia and Romanticism and Adolescence... But we cannot tell it, because it is a desire for something that has never actually appeared in our experience'.[9]

Such longing is certainly powerful: as Simone Weil has said, the reality of this hunger is not a belief but a certainty. It is also widespread, even if not universal, and it is by no means just the preserve of the privileged few: i.e. those who happen to have the heightened sensibility of a poet or the luxury of developing such feelings because they already have the basic necessities of life. The writer Penelope Fitzgerald ponders this when she considers her own homesickness. It is only a 'small wretchedness' compared to others, she says, but she still mentions it precisely because it is a small window into something similar in the experience of the truly deprived. It is intimately connected 'to the haunting faces of the [truly] displaced...and rejected...[those who] even before they set out on life's journey...seem weary already of the way... the children now who are homesick without ever having had a home to remember'.[10] In other words, this inconsolable longing is not merely self-indulgent nostalgia: it is something which relates us to others, helps us understand others in need, projects forward as much as backwards, and makes us long that the needs shall be met. It is a memory of the future as much as of the past, and a potentially ethical one.

Another place where we might trawl for signs is the sheer fact

Life Beyond Death

of creativity. This too can be seen as a sign of transcendence. George Steiner analyses creative experience like this. It is not just creating out of ourselves, but also responding to something which has come from beyond ourselves. In creativity something grasps the poet or the artist through their experience and helps give meaning to their experience, but it is not reducible to their experience. In other words, in artistic creation we do not just *create* meaning, truth, beauty, purpose – as some post-modernists would have it. Instead, we are also *responding* to meaning which is coming to us from beyond. This can be supported by listening carefully to what the most creative people actually say when they articulate their creativity. They are generally opposed to the idea that there is nothing to connect with beyond our own self-created meanings. Instead they insist they are wanting what they have created to find real connection with what lies outside themselves, some real answering response. They insist that their creativity is precisely a drive to connect with and respond to something else beyond. This in turn begs the critical question: what is it, ultimately, to which they are connecting and responding? Is it just the presence of other finite creations around them, or is it an even more profound and 'ultimate' presence?[11]

We could also turn to the discourse of natural science to look at the world it depicts. Here too a world is increasingly described which sometimes seems to point beyond itself: a world which wants further categories of explanation to help it understand itself. John Polkinghorne is one of a number of scientists who highlights features of the universe which intuitively cry out for an explanation from beyond themselves.[12] He points to the extraordinary finely tuned order and balance of the universe; or to its amazing energy of fertility and fecundity, with its constant birth and death of other stars. He then sets this alongside its transience – the ultimate death of ourselves and probably of our universe – and points out the paradox this presents: namely, we have a finely tuned and fruitful universe which is condemned to ultimate futility. It is the perception of this as a paradox, rather than just as brute fact, which is so interesting. It is like humour. It is something which doesn't fit. There is a gap, and so we need to 'mind the gap'. This is not a gap *within* scientific explanation which might soon be filled by new knowledge, but a gap opened up by the limited *kind* of explanation that science can give – and so it needs something from a different order of reality to provide it. It is, therefore, another sort of sign of transcendence.

All this enquires into natural experiences and perceptions of life for pointers to what might lie beyond it. It doesn't yield specific beliefs about life after death, but it is a context in which such beliefs may become more credible. And it all emerges without needing any particular focus on the experience of death itself – forestalling any jibe that we are only dreaming these dreams because we fear death.

Yet death remains to be pondered – even if we do not have to rely on it. So what *can* be said of it? Does death itself also lead us beyond itself?

In his study of death in the world's religions, John Bowker offers an overview of the huge variety of responses to death in different cultures and contexts. As already indicated, this shows that some religions do not include beliefs in life after death at all. Nor do they all appeal to notions of rewards, punishment or compensation as a rationale for that belief. Many are simply concerned with how death helps re-evaluate this life. Nonetheless, they almost all interpret death as 'sacrifice', and this proves fertile ground to plough. For amongst the varied meanings of sacrifice there is usually one vital common notion, which then becomes a very interesting sign of transcendence. It is the idea that sacrifice dignifies death by seeing it, in some way, as a pathway to new life and further meaning. In other words, when traditional cultures and religions have called death 'sacrifice', death is not just being seen as an outrage and an enemy to be feared – it is also seen as a necessary condition through which life can be regenerated. In fact this is something we now know about in other ways as well. We know it to be scientifically rooted in biological reality. We know, for example, that the ageing process which ultimately kills us is the same process which matures us to a point where procreation and new life is possible. We also know it is rooted in cosmological and evolutionary reality. The process by which stars and species change and die is the same process which allows complexity and other new life to emerge, and perhaps that is the only way it could emerge. So as Bowker says, 'there could not be a you, and there could not be a universe...without the death of stars and the death of succeeding generations of organic life'; and 'if you ask "why is death happening to me (or anyone)?"...' the answer has to be simply 'because you are an event of the universe; you are a child of the stars, as well as of your parents, and you could not be a child [nor anyone else] in any other way'...'[13] In short, by seeing death as purposeful sacrifice, many religious views of death had intuitively grasped long ago what scientific theory now readily confirms.

What this particularly brings into focus is how death heightens our perception of the value of life. For if the cost of all new life (i.e. sacrificial death) is so great, this spotlights the extraordinary meaning and value of the life that has come about in this way. When all life has been bought through the death of others, all life itself assumes extraordinary meaning. It assumes a kind of holiness. In other words, this perception of death as sacrifice is not just a way of describing a structure of the way things are, the bare fact that life comes through death just as 'one damn thing follows another'. It does much more. It focuses us on all that makes life so charged with meaning. It reminds us of the extraordinary textures of human awareness – our loves, dreams, aspirations, our unique thoughts, feelings, relationships. Sacrifice expresses the poignancy that *all this* is what comes about through death, as well as the fact that it is all this which is lost at death.

This in turn implies a meaning to life which 'must' be more than just being a brief bit-part in a natural sequence. After all, such a sense of profound value which sacrifice evokes challenges the very sequence of transience in which it is enmeshed. Put another way, the value of what has come about through the cost of death is too great just to die with its own death. So it raises this inescapable question: if what comes about through these natural sequences of biological birth and death has a depth of meaning which seems to transcend those processes, *where does this further meaning come from?* It seems we are back by another route to George Steiner's real presences. In the presence of life which comes about through sacrifice, we are not just trying to create meaning for it but responding to an extraordinary transcendent meaning.

This is something we sense particularly when we encounter deliberate self-sacrifice – in war or peace. It moves us profoundly, and makes us wonder deeply. But in fact doesn't *any* death move us like this? All death can move us to think that life cannot end just with this endless sequence of transience. This in turn may even point to a new kind of life which no longer depends on the endless process of more death and more sacrifice. Does it point to a sacrifice to end all sacrifices? Is this perhaps the meaning of Christ's death and resurrection?

This, of course, begins to anticipate the next chapter. It will move us out of the realm of what might be called general revelation into the world of specific Christian claims. For now I only want to have established this much. First, it matters at least to try to speak of what lies beyond this life, in spite of the limits of language. It matters because fidelity to Christian belief requires it to illuminate this world, as much as the next, and it matters simply to give hope. So, secondly, we *have* begun to speak of it – however tentatively. We have looked first for signs of transcendence in ordinary experience – and found them. They are all about us, and within us, in our sense of order, play, longing, creativity, death and sacrifice. In such ways it is possible to find, as Milan Kundera said, 'that certain part of us all that lives outside of time'. Graced nature really does yield some signs of eternity, however ambivalently, and we have to reckon with them.

Chapter 2

THE CRISIS OF DEATH AND THE CREDIBILITY OF THEISM

Signs of transcendence and intimations of immortality are written into ordinary life: in our sense of order and play, in our sense of humour and hope, in our sense of incompleteness and longing. They point to a beyondness in things. Such signs are also written into the nature of death as sacrifice – the fact that death always leads to further life for others, and thereby gives such costly meaning to life that we begin to see its infinite value. In short, these signs of hope are found in the deep structures of both life and death. They are ambivalent – they do not *have* to be seen theologically, as signs of a God who gives us afterlife, but they can point to it. That has been the argument so far.

The last point must be stressed much more before taking the argument further. Yes, such signs exist – but they are very ambivalent. They may be suggestive, but they certainly do not compel belief. They could be likened to birdsong. As with signs of transcendence, birdsong is sometimes there to be heard, hauntingly, suggestively. Occasionally, often at liminal moments like dawn, it is a glorious full chorus and it feels wholly compelling, lifting even a sceptic to a state of wistfulness if not to full belief. Just as Thomas Hardy, hearing the darkling thrush, was briefly persuaded of 'some hope whereof he knew, though I was unaware'. But it isn't always like this. Sometimes the world is just dark and silent, and at other times the song is only barely there – muted, sporadic, almost indistinguishable from other sounds of the world around. At such times we easily become sceptical, tough-minded, and reinterpret what we heard – or thought we heard. Was it really *song* at all? In biological terms, as we may remember, the birds were not singing because they had eternity set in their hearts – they were just shouting to defend their territory! It is much the same with all these signs of transcendence. They are intermittent, and easily deconstructed: they may just be the projection of our own wants and needs, rather than a reflection of something really beyond us.

So they do not convince everyone – and in the celebrated words of one philosopher it is often unbelief which seems more compelling. It seems more certain, wrote Bertrand Russell, 'that [man's] origin, his growth, his hopes and fears, his loves and beliefs, are but the outcome of accidental collocations of atoms. . .[more certain] that all the labours of the ages, all the devotion, all the inspiration, all the noonday brightness of human genius, are destined to extinction in the vast death of the solar system. . .'[1] Russell is not alone. Many of us will know what it is to meet not birdsong but just the 'blank face' of the world (as theologian Karl Rahner describes it), or 'utter silence' (as mystic philosopher Simone Weil puts it). It is because this silence from beyond is just as real as the signs of hope, that I need to say more about it. It is part of the background in which belief has to be forged and in which a specifically theological imperative will be needed.

It is a silence which can take different forms. Most obviously, as with Russell, it seems like simple absence – atheism. There simply is no God and no life beyond this life. But mention of Simone Weil reminds us that silence can also be heard as from God – but a God of such transcendence or mystery that this too seems like silence. This is often the experience of the mystics, where God's transcendence overwhelms any possibility of knowing *what* we are hearing, or not hearing. It means that the claim to hear any specific notion, like that of personal life beyond death, is somehow presumptuous.

For some there is also a silence about life beyond death even when the voice of God in other respects is quite clear and specific. Right within the Hebrew origins of our own Judaeo-Christian faith there is this sort of reticence. As Jewish scholar Alan Segal says: 'the earliest parts of the [Hebrew] Bible simply are not concerned with any life after death worth having'.[2] Instead, we are just required to ponder our days now: 'the days of our life are seventy years, or perhaps eighty if we are strong; even then their span is only toil and trouble; they are soon gone and we fly away. . .so – *teach us to count our days*'.[3] Although there was some belief in a shadowy and temporary afterlife – Sheol, the place of the spirits – this was little more than nothingness, certainly not a reality to be desired. Even when other beliefs later gained ground, this strand of silence remained. So there can be a radical silence about life after death *even within a community of faith.*

The reasons for these silences depend on the different worlds we inhabit. Russell's silence came in context of scientific rationalism. The mystics' comes in the context of God's mystery. In the world of early Hebrew religion it was perhaps the context of religious pluralism: i.e. because other religions talked freely of otherworldly spirits and ancestors, Israel needed to put down a distinctive marker – to show that monotheism had no truck with all that. As for the context of our own world, it was sketched out in the previous chapter. Our current social context has many ways of suppressing these sounds and signs of transcendence, and causing belief to decline.

We also have to face up to another reason for silence about afterlife. There is another overarching reason which runs as a common thread through all these different worlds. It is simply the fact that death appears to be such an absolute limit, such a unique and uncrossable boundary. As such it 'frames' this life, giving huge significance to what is *in* the frame (i.e. this life alone) just as any good picture frame concentrates the attention to what is within – but thereby separating that from anything which might be beyond. In other words, although I argued in the last chapter that the sacrificial nature of death may help us look beyond it, it is also the nature of death to do the opposite. The starkness of its boundary also stops us in our tracks and makes us count more carefully our days here and now.

One of the greatest western philosophers of death who took this sort of view was the twentieth-century German Martin Heidegger. Because death is this sort of boundary it fills this life with meaning – but that is all. For Heidegger this is actually a positive thing. To know that we have this frame and boundary to our lives helps us unify and integrate our lives. This is better than imagining them spread out in a prospect of endless time and change, which would leave us disintegrated. In this way death even becomes a sort of desired end. It certainly needs to be an *end*.

In what will follow, I shall want to take issue with much of what Heidegger says. With Augustine I see an orientation to eternity to be a better and truer way to unify our lives than an orientation to death. Above all, I do not see death so easily as something which neatly unifies a life – especially untimely death. Death is just as likely to tear meaning apart, whenever it happens. It often leaves unfulfilled dreams and loves both in those who die and those who are left. That is why death is often *not* 'nothing at all', as in Scott Holland's unfairly quoted text, and certainly not the giver of meaning. Instead, as Holland himself said in his full text, it can be 'the supreme and irrevocable disaster [which] makes all we do here meaningless and empty... a cruel ambush into which we are snared'.[4] It can be a boundary which shatters meaning rather than unifies it.

Yet I think we have to accept at least the overall point that Heidegger is making. Whether death neatly frames life and gives it meaning, or whether it tears it apart, this unique boundary can rub our noses back into this life, rather than leading us on to another. The possibility of seeing sacrificial death as pointing beyond itself remains, but like all the other signs death must also be seen as a very ambivalent one. It is just as likely to contribute to silence from beyond the grave as to hint at any sound of singing. *And so the case for a different kind of sign grows.* If we are going to sustain or revive belief in the face of such a stark boundary of death we shall need something much more per-suasive. The ambivalent signs of general experience, in life and death, set a scene, but they do not provide the whole narrative. Something else is clearly needed.

This now provides the context for what I want to call the *theological* imperative. That is, it signals the need to look at belief which arises specifically from the Christian revelation of the character of God, not just from general experience. As such, this will certainly require a specific dimension of *faith* but this doesn't mean just private faith, for by using the term theological I mean a belief which arises from a corporate and public faith. It is something which arises from a long, dynamic tradition and history of tested, shared, faith experience, and reflection. That, after all, is exactly the nature of theology: it is a cumulative reflection on many shared faith stories and experiences, and as such it provides its own kind of authority. And so that is the way I will now chart it first: i.e. by a historical survey of this persistent, public, theological tradition of belief in afterlife – and some of the driving forces behind it.

I will begin with the hopes of Hebrew religion. For this *has* been a cradle of positive beliefs, in spite of its early reticence about afterlife and its continuing strands of silence, and its influence is undoubted. The psalms, for example, certainly helped nourish hope. Although some psalmists have taught us only to think of our days here on earth, others have wanted to take us beyond. Thus one psalmist, perplexed by the injustices of life, enters the Temple and receives this vision: 'My flesh and my heart may fail. But God is the strength of my heart and my portion *for ever. . .*'; 'you guide me with your counsel, *and afterwards you will receive me in glory*'.[5] As one commentator puts it, he has been 'grasped by a power that even death, and the dissolution of the body, cannot thwart'.[6] Prophets also began to fill out the vision. Here is Isaiah's apocalypse for example: 'we have won no victories on earth, and no-one is born to inhabit the world. [So] your dead shall live, their corpses shall rise. O dwellers in the dust, awake and sing for joy! For your dew is a radiant dew, and the earth will give birth to those long dead'.[7] This may be a vision only of Israel's collective restoration at some future time in earthly history, rather than a specific belief in personal afterlife. But when Daniel meditated later on it, it surely includes personal afterlife: 'many of those who sleep in the dust of the earth shall awake, some to everlasting life, and some to everlasting shame and contempt'.[8] We should also note that this is not just a general longing: it is a specific form of belief which suggests that we are to be recreated out of dust like our first creation for some specific purpose (in this case for reward and punishment).

What was driving this expression of hope? There were probably some influences from Zoroastrian beliefs in life after death, encountered in the exile period. Perhaps some imagery was also borrowed from Greek philosophy, from Plato or Cicero (Daniel, for example, later uses the Greek image of shining stars to picture immortality). But I doubt that these foreign images were the main driving force behind the belief itself, because they were coming from what was a largely enemy or alien culture. The more obvious impetus to the belief was closer to hand in their more immediate context, which was the ferocious persecution of the period – the Maccabean martyrdoms when the pious were being slaughtered and justice was simply not prevailing in this life alone. In other words it was the requirement of divine justice which shaped this hope – just as it did with the psalmist in the Temple. Some life beyond this one was required to fulfil justice.

Other theological and moral motors were also operating. For instance, it is likely that a prior belief in divine creation was also playing a part. The image of re-forming people after death out of 'the dust of the ground' is a clear echo of the first creation story. It suggests that some sense of the sheer vitality of divine creation was helping shape the belief. Such divine creativity simply cannot accept the extinction of what it makes, and so it must always look to renew or recreate it.

Most of all the belief in afterlife was being driven by belief in divine faithfulness: i.e. God's faithfulness to His own covenant. As each period of exile, persecution, setback ensued, the pressure grew to show how God's promises to Israel could be vindicated, how God's faithfulness could be credible. How this was conceived – whether it meant the restoration of Israel in this world or another, and whether it specifically included restoration of life for individuals who have died – is less clear. Overall it appeared to include at least some expectation that the dead would be able to wait as spirits before a general bodily resurrection back on this earth. I shall say more about all these options in the next chapter. However, the main point I want to stress here is simply the theological motor driving all these various forms of belief: namely, the conviction of God's character as *just, creative, faithful.* Grasped by this sort of God, the issue was forced: when disaster struck and mortality knocked at the door there must be something else to happen; when the hammer of suffering and death fell on the anvil of God's justice, creativity and faithfulness, new hopes had to be forged in the furnace. For how could God's creation simply be written off? How could God's promise to His people simply be extinguished?

In this way, as Alan Segal says, we see a form of argument going on in this theological history. It is an argument from the nature of God and this world to the hope of a world beyond. This is not an argument in purely rational form: i.e. 'if God is just then He must 'logically' recreate us in some new way'. The belief is given as visionary perception in the heat of dire events, and only later elaborated as argument. Nonetheless, it is argument, both with God and about God – as authentic theology often is!

What happens when we move on in theological history into the New Testament era? We move above all, of course, to the pivotal event of Jesus Christ – which came into, and arose out of, just this varied background of beliefs. It was an event, therefore, which was mediated in a context both of some denial about resurrection, but also some robust beliefs in general bodily resurrection (and a restoration of Israel). As the event unfolded it was also increasingly shaped by Greek ideas of immortality – which had more to do with a disembodied existence in an eternal heaven, rather than bodily resurrection on a restored earth. So it was within this multi-layered context that the Christ event provided its new and extraordinary impetus.

How did it do this? A key point stressed by Tom Wright, amongst others, is that the Christ event came to be seen first (uniquely) as a resurrection that had already happened. Rather than waiting like the rest of us for a general resurrection, Christ was seen to have been raised already. 'Because Yahweh was the creator, and because he was the god of justice, [people already hoped that] the martyrs would be raised and Israel as a whole would be vindicated. But nobody imagined that any individuals had already been raised, or would be raised in advance of the great last day' (not even Elijah or Moses).[9] Yet Christ was. This did not necessarily much affect the *nature* of hope. After all, if Christ did not return before their death, they still expected that they would have a period of spiritual waiting until the general resurrection. But it better *grounded* their hope. To put it simply, since it had already happened for him they could be all the more assured it would happen for them.

In fact there are also some implications for the nature of life after death, which I will explore in the next chapter. For instance, there are questions it raises about whether we shall have to wait in time, what it means to be raised bodily, and so on (and in dealing with this I will take issue with some of Tom Wright's picture). But for now I simply want to note this primary significance of the Christ event in grounding belief in afterlife more firmly, in galvanizing the hope and giving more confidence to it. This is worth noting, not least because it is not always clear from in the actual resurrection stories of the synoptic Gospels themselves.[10] They do not say much explicitly about its significance for afterlife, and seem to use the story with other purposes in mind – such as establishing Jesus' identity and inspiring discipleship for this life. However, its effect of increasing confidence in afterlife *is* clear enough elsewhere in the overall unfolding of the event. Thus for Paul especially, afterlife for us is an essential part of the meaning of Christ's resurrection. For 'if for this life only we have hoped in Christ, we are of all people most to be pitied' – and we are not to be pitied precisely because Christ's resurrection was not just the vindication of one man for

Life Beyond Death

this life but 'the first fruits of [all] those who have died' ...[11] Here
there is no doubt: hope for our afterlife is intrinsically connected
to Christ's resurrection.

What drove the unfolding of this clear meaning? It is a
meaning drawn out of a heady and complex cocktail of ingre-
dients, both within the resurrection event itself and its surrounding context. Out of this, I suggest that two issues will
illuminate this process particularly well. First, it was another time
of persecution, chiefly from Rome. So the belief once again
gained impetus from the imperative for justice. When an out-
rageous death hammers on divine justice, belief in resurrection
takes wing – both for Christ himself, and then through him for
his faithful followers. The book of Revelation is especially vivid
about this. Resurrection is about vindication: making things right
and just – both for the lamb who was slain and for those who
followed him.

Secondly, there was another dynamic at work. There was also
the imperative of divine *love*. To some extent this was new. To
be sure, there were already profound perceptions of divine love
abroad in Hebrew thought, but in the interpretation of Christ's
resurrection new dimensions of the meaning of that love were
brought to bear. What was helping to interpret his resurrection
was the whole event of his living, teaching, passion and dying –
and from all that the meaning of divine covenant love gained
new depth. It was such a love that simply could not let him go –
or let us go. So it didn't – it raised him, and will raise us. Paul
again is the most explicit about this: there is such 'breadth and
length and height and depth' of this love '... that neither death
nor life, nor angels, nor rulers, nor things present, nor things to
come, nor powers, nor height, nor depth, nor anything else in all
creation, will be able to separate us from the love of God in
Christ Jesus our Lord'.[12] This is again a form of argument:
something born of vision and experience, but then developed as
the rhetoric of theological argument.

Thus both justice and love are major drivers in the meanings
of resurrection that unfolded – and the logic of divine creation

again also played some role. For as Paul says in his same chapter about love, it is the whole creation which God will not abandon to decay, not just you and me. *All* God makes he loves, and so cannot allow any of it to be extinguished. Thus, with this huge impetus of the Christ event, the story continued and developed. The belief encountered new influences, threaded its way though further new contexts, became reshaped, yet persisted. And even the very brief and inevitably selective journey through subsequent theological history which now follows will illustrate this persistence well.

To begin in the earliest church, the belief was often linked to an expectation of the imminent return of Christ to earth – so soon that many thought they would experience a new heaven and earth even before their death. When hopes of this receded, and with the conversion of Emperor Constantine, the church put more energy into this world and its future. Nonetheless, as the cycles of civic and political rise and fall continued, and even Rome became insecure, the vision of the Earthly City was never going to wholly supplant the Heavenly City. Belief in afterlife still retained its vigour. And this continued in medieval Christendom. It was a time when the church once more gained in this-worldly influence, yet still retained its interest in the hereafter. In fact this interest positively flourished. In both popular and scholastic thought it took wing in a kind of imaginative anarchy. The background of black death, war, famine, and more plague, created a constant threat of death which fed huge popular speculation about life beyond. At the same time the relative stability of ecclesiastical authority also gave church theologians the opportunity and energy to develop the speculation themselves, in great detail. So they did, with extraordinary vividness, in the pictures of purgatory, damnation and bliss written into the sculpture of cathedrals, in the theology of the scholastics, and in the poetry of the philosophers, and the minds of ordinary people. (If you ever doubt that there was a surplus of imaginative energy, consider Aquinas's immense efforts to refute some of the more bizarre arguments circulating at the time: e.g. the arguments to show how a cannibal who is entirely made out of the bodies of other people he has eaten, can still have enough of his own body to be raised himself!). The prime theological motors in this period were again the demands of judgement, justice, reward and punishment, but love also played its part. Mysticism in particular kept alive the imperative of love in the 'beatific vision' of God: i.e. that vision of God as all-embracing love, inexorably drawing us into a unity with Himself, which could only be ultimately fulfilled in eternity. And as for the Reformation, it helped forge yet another context, but again the preoccupation remained. Although it was actually a strong Reformation theme to value ordinary life here and now, its overall drive to rebel against corrupt worldly powers kept alive the longing for end times – to overthrow all current order. So in that sense the many reformers also *wanted* to reach an afterlife. Some of the detail of the medieval period is rejected, but not the basic hope of hereafter.

But how has the belief in afterlife fared in our own more recent theological history? As we know, this is a theological history which has had to adapt to even more major intellectual and social changes. There has been the rise of scientific rationalism and biblical criticism, then romanticism with its appeal to feelings, intuition, subjectivity. It is a history relating to a world of industrial and technological progress which first seemed to make it possible to bring heaven to earth in material progress, sanitation, medicine, and so on – but which has also brought hell to earth in industrialized war, environmental decay, global uncertainties. More recently – in what we now call post-modernity – it is a theological history being shaped through the melting pot of a society where we dip randomly into fragments of *all* these past religious, rational, romantic ideas to try and make sense of our beliefs, but no longer feel we can trust any one overall story, whether Biblical, scientific, or political. So – how has theology dealt with belief in afterlife through all this?

The belief has certainly been reshaped. It has sometimes been sidelined, sometimes radically shaken, but on the whole it has again still persisted. To begin with, amongst the so-called liberal protestants of the nineteenth century, the early progress of science undoubtedly focussed theology much more on God's Kingdom in human achievement here and now. But the first world war then changed that theological agenda – as surely as September 11th 2001 may be changing it now. For in the wake of the war, the idea that God could be so easily limited to human achievement in human history seemed incredible, even absurd. Swiss theologian Karl Barth in particular launched a massive assault on such an idea. He reasserted both the transcendence of God and the uniqueness of the Christ event. Instead of looking for God's Kingdom in general human history, he looked for it only in the Christ event – and came to believe that God's transcendent eternity could only contain human history in so far as our history is 'strained' through Christ. As every grain of sand in an hourglass has to pass through one small point to reach its destiny, all of this world has to pass through Christ into eternity – yet, by God's transcendent power and grace, and through Christ, all *can* pass through. So in the end, although Barth has little to say explicitly about afterlife for individuals, he was implicitly a radical universalist. This turned out to be an overall stance characteristic of many other theologians affected by war, even though they did not share Barth's wider theology. With hell so present in the here and now of war, heaven hereafter must be more widely available than most church teaching of the past had suggested. On the moral mess of the battlefield, chaplains especially found they could no longer restrict hope for the few, ring-fence it with theological niceties such as the protestant dogma about justification by faith alone, or catholic dogma about salvation only in the church.[13] If life after death was on offer at all it would have to be for *all*, even the enemy. As the poet Wilfred Owen said before he died, if Christ was anywhere he was in no man's land, not just on one side or another.

Other more recent atrocities have had different effects. Auschwitz produced some theology which was just searing protest against *any* belief in afterlife. Afterlife was written out of belief altogether for fear that any notion of eternity trivializes the evil of suffering. There was a terror of suggesting that suffering could somehow be compensated, or even justified, by eternity. These theologies have directed us instead to a God who only suffers with us in the here and now, rather than the transcendent God of eternity rescuing us from it. In Bonhoeffer's celebrated phrase 'only a *suffering* God can help' – and so a God beyond this life and an afterlife fall out of focus altogether (though not for Bonhoeffer himself). It is a theological trend reinforced by the general turn inwards of contemporary culture: the attempt to redefine God just within our own feelings and spirituality. But it is certainly not the only reaction. Other theologies, equally borne out of suffering, have resisted this conclusion. They remind us that a God who is *only* with us here and now in this life is precisely the one who cannot help enough. Only if God also has a foothold in eternity can he help us fully. Only a God beyond as well as within this life is credible *as God*. Frances Young, for example, has reflected on her own experience with her incurably handicapped son, to find that it is the eternal and transcendent God, existing beyond time and passion, who spoke to her clearly and gave her credible hope, not just the immanent suffering God.[14]

There has been a similar dialogue within feminist theologies. Some see preoccupation with death and what is beyond as a typically male preoccupation. They suggest it should be replaced by the female focus on birth, life and embodiment here and now. Rather than seeing death as the gateway to our own survival, we should see it as a way of giving space for others to be born and live: by death we give ourselves back to the womb of the natural world, to nourish the new birth of others from our bodily decay – a sort of theology of recycling.[15] It is a way of accepting the sacrificial meaning of death for others which I have already referred to, but without taking the further step of seeing that sacrifice pointing also to the *infinite* value of life. Other feminist theologians take a different view. They are adamant that to see death in this way limits human hope unnecessarily. They suggest that it owes more to ecological ideologies preoccupied with limited natural resources, than to a Christian theology of God's unlimited resources which can take us beyond this life.[16]

A similar oscillation runs through recent theology influenced by post-modern concerns with narrative. These are attempts to understand how the shape of stories illuminates the meaning of our lives. The suspicion of post-modernity is that by thinking of life as an overall story heading to some 'completion' or 'fulfilment' (such as heaven), we will close down options: i.e. the story prescribes where we are heading, making any meaning in the present only provisional. So we are encouraged to find all meaning instead in the flux of each passing present moment, not some distant promised end. Rather than looking forward to a future wholeness, rather than saying with King Lear that 'ripeness is all', the great virtue is to be more like children for whom 'this present moment is all' (certainly a more popular view in current culture generally!). Post-modern theology which takes this on board will simply sack heaven – and it reduces to another of those silences about heaven we find even within the faith tradition. But again, it is not the only story. There are others who have offered a different response to the demands of narrative. It is quite possible to have a more nuanced view of heaven. Eternity does not have to mean the kind of completion which closes down options. As I will suggest in chapter four, there are some kinds of completions to stories which are not final endings but gateways to new possibilities. So in fact this narrative take on theology can open up a belief in afterlife rather than close it down – another example of how the belief persists in theological history, through all its changing contexts.

Even this short and selective tour of theological history is therefore enough to demonstrate the resilience of the belief. It has been reshaped in different contexts, but like Blake's golden thread it is still woven through it all. Even if it has faltered in more recent times, there is no overall pattern which suggests it is heading inexorably in just one direction. And so this sort of historical approach to theology sets its agenda and offers its imperative. It provides at least a *prima facie* case to sustain the belief now as much as ever. For if it has persisted through so many contexts, shouldn't we be willing to reshape it in ours, rather than quietly giving it up? It should challenge that reticence about the belief we now find amongst the faithful. It should also challenge reticence amongst those who are actually teaching and preaching in churches, and in the training of clergy (where, we are told, there is much good training on pastoral counselling for the bereaved, but not always much to do with the theology of eternity!).[17]

Moreover, there is another dimension to this imperative. For what this historicist way of doing theology uncovers is not just the resilience of the belief through time. It also showed clearly how this belief is always woven into key features of God's character and identity: God's justice, love, creativity and transcendent capacity to save. So it shows the inextricable relation of this belief to other foundational beliefs about a personal God, and this draws us into another way of doing theology and finding its imperatives. This is the way of systematic theology: i.e. the attempt to look at the *coherence* of its beliefs as a whole, not just their individual linear development.

As mentioned in the introduction, this is not a fashionable way of doing anything these days. Anything which smacks of a rational system or 'package' of belief is widely regarded with scepticism. But it is important to make clear what I mean here by a systematic approach – and what I do not mean. For a start, I do not mean that to devise a rational connection between beliefs will itself be compelling, or that true belief only emerges as a property of some tightly bound rational system. It is clear that belief in afterlife does not follow 'logically' simply from belief in a good creator God (neither Job nor Jesus in Gethsemane found truth or faith in that sort of way). Nor do I mean that what people actually believe is always systematic. Beliefs which are theologically connected may still be psychologically quite separable. It is clearly possible for people in their actual experience of faith to separate belief in God from belief in life after death. As we have seen, some in Israel clearly believed one without the other, and some people do now, for the reasons I have already acknowledged. They retain deep faith in God without hope beyond this life. This is an austere faith, but faith nonetheless. Arguably it is a magnificent faith – to 'trust in God though he slay me'. However – none of this implies that connections and coherence have no significance at all. Even if beliefs are not bound together by logical or psychological necessity, the appeal to general coherence still has considerable suggestive force. Connections and coherence in beliefs about God which emerge through shifting time and experience do still matter. For if God has any sort of identifiable character He will not be entirely incoherent and inconsistent. Even as a mysterious, free and transcendent God, He will not be wholly capricious. In that sense He is bound to make Himself known at least partly through some of our 'systems' of thought and our connected patterns of experience.

In this sense, therefore, we *should* allow ourselves to think systematically – and if we do, it certainly adds weight to this belief. For think what happens when we reflect in a connected way on all that has emerged in theological history. Reflect on the power of divine creativity, the urgency of divine justice, the dynamic of divine love and faithfulness; reflect on the passion of generosity and love experienced in Christ's cross and resurrection. Reflect also on the actual nature of human experience in this wondrous but achingly bloody and incomplete world, in which the longing is never satisfied. Then reflect on all that *together* to try to make sense of it. The theological mind and imagination will be driven inevitably to afterlife. We are bound to conclude that for divine justice, creativity, and love to have full meaning, the world's evils 'must' be redeemed beyond what we see. Otherwise it would not be a perfect justice and creativity or a credible love. I repeat, the force of this 'must' is neither purely logical nor psychological: but it is fully theological. As Michael Ramsey says more simply: the meaning of humanity and of God's infinite love just 'requires' heaven. Or as a Christian poet from South America put it when living under the oppression of a dictatorship, watching countless victims walk briefly, cruelly, namelessly, into oblivion: all human life *must* be 'a door that turns into many exits ... a wave that no seashore devours ... as beautiful as the waves in the sum of their infinity'.[18] His faith and his fierce wonder and love of life have combined to make him see that life must go on. It is all part of theodicy: i.e. a systematic attempt to come to terms with suffering and injustice as a believer in a good, creative God – and finding in the process that some sort of life beyond this one is indispensable in that attempt.

This motive of theodicy is often at the heart of a systematic theology which cherishes afterlife. To be sure, it can be a flawed motive. It can imply that great evil is somehow mitigated or even justified by God's future gift of heaven. That is the kind of theodicy that Dostoevsky's character Ivan rightly nails as moral nonsense in a celebrated episode of his novel *The Brothers Karamazov*. But that is not the sort of theodicy I mean here. I do not mean using heaven to spell out how there can be a justification for suffering and evil. I mean the attempt simply to maintain the hope that suffering and evil does not have the last word. I mean the appeal to heaven as the possibility that evil can and will be redeemed in some way, even though we know not how or why. And in that general sense, theodicy's appeal to heaven *is* a proper and powerful part of this imperative. It acknowledges that heaven is critical to the credibility of a good God. It is saying that *without* heaven the credibility of a creator God of love crumbles. It is admitting that if there is nothing else for a life lived only as brief span of ache and sorrow we would have to fall silent about divine love – and we might even join hands with Russell and Ivan Karamazov and deny God altogether. But *with* this hope of heaven all changes. Divine love becomes more believable. The beatitudes become believable. Those who hunger and thirst for righteousness shall be satisfied, even when this life does not satisfy. Those who mourn shall be comforted, even when this life does not comfort them. As one writer who lost his son has said, those who mourn still ache but they can become 'aching *visionaries*' – people who can look forward in their loss, not just backwards.[19]

In both these ways, historically and systematically, theology therefore provides its imperative to believe in the next life. General religion and spirituality do not necessarily do this. It is not provided by the so-called spiritual revolution of our times – that 'turn inwards' which reduces God to our own inner spirituality and deprives us of an adequate power of transcendence. But the imperative *is* there in theism, through faith in a personal creator God who is beyond us, as well as within us. And as such it is not surprising to find that this imperative of eternity is well expressed in theism's best cradle and theology's best origin: in *worship*. After all real worship, like being in love, is bound to give us some of our sharpest insights into the 'chief end of man', what we're ultimately *for* – and what emerges in this intensity of worship (as in love) is precisely the compulsion of eternity. We find that our ultimate purpose is simply to be in a relationship with the object of our love 'for ever'. Remember, even the atheist Nietzsche had a sense of this. As he said, 'all true delight *desires eternity*'.

So that is the theological imperative for the hope of life beyond death. The next chapter will venture something about what it might be like, but thus far it has been just the fact of it that I have tried to trace: I have sketched out just the outward form of the hope which is so insistent through theological history and systematic theology. Yet even in this bare form it is clearly a hope which is no added extra but is inextricably woven into the heart of the character and credibility of God. It presses on us as a belief which arises inexorably from faith which is public, tested, corporate – and which is generated and sustained not least in a living tradition of worship. It is an imperative to believe which sounds a surer note than the birdsong of general experience, even as it resonates so well with it.

Life Beyond Death

Chapter 3

MEANINGS OF RESURRECTION

The air is full of angels. Signs of transcendence and rumours of immortality abound, not just in privileged mystical moments, but as part of the air we breathe in ordinary human experience of order, play, humour, longing. They are only ambivalent signs – always open to deconstruction, easy to interpret as something else. Yet the rumours will not go away and when we enter the specific stories of Christian faith and its theology, then the rumours gather momentum. The whispers are shouted aloud. In its hope for justice, in the resurrection story, and in the very nature of God, there is a powerful theological imperative to believe that there is more to life than this life.

That briefly summarizes the discussion so far. Now I have to ask this rather more difficult question: can we go beyond the bare belief *that* there is something beyond this life – can we say something about what it might be like? I have resisted this so far, wanting to take seriously the limits of all thought and speech about the transcendent. I want to heed Wittgenstein's dictum that 'whereof one cannot speak, one should be silent'. But it is hard completely to hold this line. After all, we have to give some content to the hope for it to have any meaning at all. So although it is difficult, even dangerous, to name our hopes (to wait with hope is almost certainly to 'wait for the wrong thing', as T. S. Eliot says), we still have to take the risk. Even Eliot himself eventually began to do this: first just in the absences of experience, in 'footfalls of the memory', in a 'door we never opened' – but then in more concrete, positive images: hope is in 'the rose garden', in 'children's laughter'.[1] It seems that some positive images are required if there is to be meaning at all in what we hope for.

They are also required to make sure we are not just left with easily discredited images like harps and thrones for heaven, or fire and brimstone for hell, or a returning Christ taking people up in a cloud into the sky. Such images have often been taken too literally, rather than symbolically, so we need to make sure they are not left as the sole occupants of the playing field. We must therefore try some re-imaging and re-conceptualizing. To prevent the baby of heaven being thrown out with its imaginative bathwater, we have to give the baby some other shape to hold onto it.

To do this is a tall order, and I shall certainly have to set some limits. In particular I will limit myself to imaging *life* beyond death, not death beyond death. In other words, I am going to explore resurrection for heaven, not resurrection for hell or extinction. I will not be dealing either with questions of judgement: i.e. the business of discerning differences in people which might justify different destinies. There is proper theological discussion to be had about all that but it is not the subject of this book. Even so, the question remains hard enough. How can eternal life be spoken of sensibly?

One way is simply to translate traditional images into their contemporary counterparts. In other words, if a heaven of harps and thrones doesn't sound plausible, substitute them with Mozart and shopping malls. Anthony DeStefano tries this in his recent best-selling *Travel Guide to Heaven*.[2] The trouble is, this hardly results in anything more convincing than the traditional images. DeStefano's heaven is described as so materially real, so like our current embodied lives on earth, that it turns out to be little more than a celestial five star resort. As one reviewer complains, heaven resembles the Presidential Suite in a Beverley Hills Hotel, wonderful sex with your spouse, good claret, and angels ministering to us like perfect tour guides. In short, life beyond death is just conceived as a state of enhanced earthly pleasures expressed in the terms of twentieth-century materialism. It merely becomes the sort of picture of life beyond death that is 'sneered at by sophisticated theologians and rubbished by unbelievers as a cynical recruitment ploy'.[3] Clearly it is not just traditional images which need care – all images carry their own risks.

Nonetheless, as I have said, we cannot do without some images – and in fact even those rather crude popular images of DeStefano's book alert us to something we cannot ignore: namely, we still need images with some continuity to present life. As the same reviewer commented, DeStefano's general notion of heaven as an embodied life with some recognizable continuity with earthly experience is actually based in a tradition of serious Christian exegesis. Tom Wright's recent work on resurrection, briefly referred to in the last chapter, is a good example. Wright makes a very strong assertion of our hopes for bodily resurrection. That is what traditional biblical doctrine does. It commits us to using images of recognizable continuity with this life – it talks of bodies as well as souls, time as well as eternity, individuals as well as 'cosmic wholes'. In short, it appears to commit us to a heaven which includes recognizable reality, at least in some sense. The theological warrant for this was touched on in the first chapter: if we are already made in this world in the image of God, then the ultimate things of God and heaven for which we are destined should have some recognizable connection with things we know in this world.

So we are bound to look for some positive images which connect with this life in some way. Yet they also need to be disciplined to make sure they are not just crude extensions of this life. So what sort of discipline? I suggest the following provides a simple, sound, rule of thumb. Whatever images we use, we need to make sure that they express the positive theological *purpose* of heaven – which, as emphasized in the previous chapter, always has to do with justice, creativity, love, and worship. To keep this in mind will at least help us avoid mere wishful thinking or self-indulgence, yet it will still allow positive, life-affirming images (rather than purely 'apophatic' negations of this life). Another theological discipline to keep firmly in mind is the pivotal event at the heart of these purposes of justice, creativity and love – namely, the resurrection. We should always look for the shape that resurrection gives to our images of justice and love beyond death. And since this last point – i.e. resurrection as the hermeneutical key to our images of belief – lies at the heart of Tom Wright's book *The Resurrection of the Son of God*, this provides a good place to start (even if we need to go beyond it in due course). What then, according to Wright, is the specific shape of the resurrection hope?

Both Jewish and early Christian understandings of resurrection included the following characteristics. First, resurrection definitely involved embodiment. We should not expect to survive as disembodied souls or spirits as our ultimate end: instead we are to become re-embodied persons, in some sense. Secondly, what happens beyond death involved a further narrative, a further story to our lives. We should expect to experience new events in some sort of continuing passage of time and change. There will be various stages in this further story: immediately after death there is a disembodied state for a while as we wait for the end of all things; then there is resurrection in which we are all re-embodied, then we can expect still further story to unfold. Thirdly, there was the expectation of some sort of new environment, a place to be. There will be a new earth for our new life, not just some placeless spiritual dimension entirely beyond space and time. Heaven (i.e. God's dwelling) might be like that, but for Wright we do not hope to go to 'heaven'. Our destiny is new earth which God comes *from* heaven to remake for us.

That is Wright's broad understanding about the nature of resurrection in its Jewish background and earliest Christian form. It means that those who die now enter an intermediate spiritual state, but then at some future time they are raised with a new body for a new life on a new earth. It is a picture drawn directly from some of the core, recurring images of scripture, some of which were mentioned in the previous chapter: e.g. Isaiah's apocalypse, and Daniel, which speak of the dead who have been 'waiting', then being 'raised from the dust and given new bodies'. It is also drawn from Gospel narratives of Christ's resurrection, and from Paul's picture (e.g. in Thessalonians) where the risen Lord will come from heaven to meet those already dead, who then rise to be with him on the new earth.

This basic shape could also be filled out a little further – again, just by staying faithfully with some core early biblical images and teaching. So we could go on to say that resurrection life will certainly be more desirable than this life: for 'there will be no more mourning or crying or pain' (Revelation) and 'to die is gain', it is to be 'with Christ' (Paul). It will involve change, because we shall have an imperishable 'spiritual' body (perhaps something like Jesus' own changed resurrection body), yet in spite of the change we may also hope to remain as recognizable, named, persons – just as the risen Jesus was still identifiable. Equally, we are not raised with individual names alone: it seems we are always raised with others, to be with God and to praise God together. This may be because we are so connected to each other and the rest of creation that we cannot be fulfilled alone: 'apart from others none of us can be made perfect' (to paraphrase Hebrews). This may be why we are described as having to 'wait' for the general resurrection.

All these are biblical images which give some definitive shape to the hope. It is a shape which fits well enough with those overall theological purposes of the belief. After all, to be re-embodied and recognizable, as well as changed, means we can imagine enjoying personal relations with each other and God, rather than losing our identity altogether as indistinguishable drops in an ocean. That in turn allows us to imagine how love and justice could be perfected in eternity. For love always requires some distinction between persons, not complete merging (an insight which fits well with later trinitarian theology that sees God like this in His own eternity: i.e. as a dynamic relationship of interpenetrating but distinct persons, living out a continuing narrative of love within His own being). It is an overall shape to the hope which also fits well with the purposes of divine creation. After all, images which ask us to think of ourselves re-embodied on a re-made earth make it easier to see this creation is in some way continuing and valued, not just something to be dismissed as a dispensable preliminary to something wholly new.

Such are some basic pictures and concepts we might draw from core biblical resurrection images – if we confine ourselves to them in this largely uncritical and phenomenological way. But I have to ask: is it sufficient just to provide a faithful retrieval of some core biblical images in this way? What about the way they have developed in the subsequent tradition? What about their interaction with other thought? And above all what do we really *mean* by 'some kind of re-embodiment', and 'waiting' for a 'new earth' with continuing 'time' and history? If we are going to make any meaning of these basic images in a way which is imaginable and plausible in our own world view we shall surely need to explore them further – whatever the perils.

To begin with this means looking at those developing theological traditions and the way images moved beyond from these Hebraic origins. This in turn means we must begin with the way in which Greek thought increasingly played a part and helped developed new images. This is not to imply that there was ever a 'pure' Hebrew world accessible to us, which Christian tradition then developed with other ideas in straightforward linear fashion. The Hebrew thought expressed in biblical literature was already a complex recipient of other influences, including Greek ones. Nonetheless, to help identify the various dominant strands in the traditions, it is still useful to separate them conceptually. There are broad differences in emphasis between Hebrew and Greek thought, as well as some more nuanced coalitions, and the way these distinct traditions have interrelated is instructive.

A first major distinction in the development of Christian belief relates to its anthropology (i.e. what it means to be human). It is a familiar point that Greek thinking generally distinguished more sharply between body and soul than the Hebrew understanding of ourselves as a unified body and soul. In contrast to Hebrew ideas, Greek thought conceived the soul to be separable, an immortal spark imprisoned within the body in this life, then freed at death to return to its timeless and eternal home. This meant that death seemed less of a complete barrier and more just a mechanism of release for that essential part of us which naturally lives on. So whereas Hebrew anthropology led early Christian ideas of resurrection to mean first a total end at bodily death, and only later a re-creation at the general resurrection, Greek anthropology allowed a more seamless continuity: the soul just moved on. This is one reason, perhaps, why Socrates could apparently face his death with equanimity, in contrast to Jesus who trembled in distress (though one could think of other reasons for this too!).

These notions of an immortal soul certainly entered Christian understanding, in spite of their differences with Hebrew anthropology. They quickly combined with images of resurrection. It is easy to see why. Conceptually it was useful to have the clear notion of a soul which could exist on its own because it helped explicate that time of disembodied waiting before the general bodily resurrection. It was also existentially attractive. It is comforting to think that a vital part of our being simply continues at death, rather than facing the prospect of a complete ending, and only later a return to life. It is reassuring to think death is, in that sense, 'nothing at all'. And this attraction has persisted. Although the existence of a separable soul is hard to prove and easy to dismiss (especially in a more materialist age), it is also hard to *dis*prove – and it certainly retains some hold in popular imagination both outside and within the churches. In the survey of beliefs quoted in the first chapter, you may remember, only very few churchgoers believed in bodily resurrection, but many more believed in survival of the soul. The general turn inwards of contemporary culture which I also mentioned can reinforce this. It is a climate in which people are more likely to think in terms of some aspect of their own subjective spirituality surviving, rather than relying on some objective God re-making them from beyond. In one way or another, therefore, this 'soul language' of Greek influence has clearly been fertile – and may still be.

A similar story can be told of Greek cosmology (i.e. its

understanding of the wider universe), especially its views of time and eternity. These also attached themselves quickly to early Christian belief, in spite of some contrast with Hebrew cosmology. In Hebrew thought time was held to be real in a largely linear, common sense way: that is, it moved you forward from one thing to another in a forward journey. This was not the whole Hebrew picture of time – key events like the Passover held a sort of transcendence, as if they could be revisited in some way. Nonetheless, overall time was still expected to move us ever forward to new things, which was also expected to continue in the new heaven and earth. As Wright says, it would be a continued forward-moving *narrative*. In contrast, Greek cosmology (especially Plato's) viewed forward moving time as largely unreal, just a broken shadow of an ultimate destiny which would be a timeless eternity. Yet in spite of this difference Christian theology again readily assimilated this Greek view into its afterlife. From Augustine to Boethius, in the platonic tradition of the early western church to the English imagination of the metaphysical poets like Henry Vaughan and John Donne, we have a dominant strand of images of heaven which are much more like a Greek eternity: 'no ends nor beginnings but one equal eternity'.[4] There are also traces of platonism in some of the nineteenth-century hymns which most caught the twentieth-century imagination: '*Abide with me*', for example, tells us that 'heaven's morning breaks and earth's vain shadows flee'. These are the shadows of time and change which flee, as the *un*changing God takes us to a heaven out of time.

In such ways, Greek influence has clearly contributed persuasive images, in spite of its contrasts. It has been exceptionally influential in mainstream western theology for centuries – and as I've indicated, it can still capture imagination in popular theology and culture. So is it worth exploring further?

We shall see. But first we must reckon with the fact that much western theology of the last century actually turned against it and tried to oust it – for powerful reasons. These are mostly to do with those underlying contrasts with Hebrew thought and their

Life Beyond Death

implications – which have broken surface more readily in changing historical circumstances, and which have come to seem unsustainable. Theologians have generally become much more wary of any world view which fails to take death seriously as a real end and enemy; wary of anything that might downgrade our bodies and this material world and thereby diminish the significance of creation and incarnation; wary of a world view which thinks it can conceive of a soul apart from body and brain (especially in the light of recent medical science); and wary of any view which thinks that personal life could ever exist in a timeless and changeless state and remain recognizably personal. Cumulatively these concerns have led to a major theological consensus to eject what it sees as the Greek cuckoo from the Judaeo-Christian nest: to decontaminate itself from Greek ideas and stay closer to the Hebrew mind-set, especially when imaging afterlife.

However, although all this might lead us to think that the Greek turn was simply a blind alley, I do not think we can leave it there. This is for two kinds of reasons. Firstly, I do not believe that Greek thought was so fruitless. Secondly, even if it was, I do not think it is enough to restate Hebrew imagery instead, as if its own underlying anthropology and cosmology (and theology) have no problems themselves. I will take this second point first: i.e. to explain further why I do not think we can resort to those core resurrection biblical images and say no more.

We need to consider more carefully what these images actually give us, just in their own terms. The basic shape is a story of spiritual waiting, then re-embodiment in a resurrection body for new life together with God on a re-created new earth. But is that really sufficient to help us think plausibly about what is truly transcendent? By telling a time-bound story of our bodies on this earth, it may be inclined to tie us too much to our current experience of time, space, and matter. Just the words 'body' and 'earth' are strong, gritty, images which rub us in the present reality of what *is*: they do not easily release our imagination to travel beyond the texture of this actual stuff of which we now know we are made and which we now inhabit. That stuff is in fact a bio-chemical reality, rooted on this planet, which in the end we know to be transient, cooling matter thrown out by exploding stars, all destined for death. Admittedly, the biblical language is intending to refer us to a *new* body on a *new* earth – but on its own this still gives no real imaginative force to the newness. As I have insisted, this does not mean we need to purge our images of all sense of continuity (and I certainly do not want to dispense with all images of body, earth, time): but it does mean we may need to develop them in other ways as well, and relate them to other conceptualities.

There are at least two ways in which we can do this. The first is from the biblical tradition itself. We need to give more weight to other themes as well – those which *do* help give force to that radical newness which is required. For instance, there are the prophecies of Isaiah and the apocalypse of Revelation, where we find more clearly the hope for God to do a radically new thing. This is conveyed especially by their specific talk of divine re-creation. For whenever God *creates* this is always a radical act: it is not just an extension of Himself or derivation, or repetition, or recycling; it is not the spurious novelty of the sort we are so familiar with in our commercialised world. Instead, divine creation always includes real difference as well as some continuity; otherness as well as connection. The apocalyptic language in which new creation in the Bible is sometimes couched reinforces this. It is deliberately extravagant, vivid language, throwing up wonderful juxtapositions, oxymorons, impossible contradictions: 'a *lion* lying down with a *lamb*, a *life* where there is no more *death*, a *love* where there is no more mourning or pain, a *body* which is *incorruptible*'... and so on. In our current experience these could only be dreams and imaginative fantasies – but that is precisely why they are used: i.e. to drive us to conceive of something truly new, truly transcendent. In a fine discussion of biblical images and fantasy Richard Bauckham and Trevor Hart say just this: '[these] statements are, due to their deliberate and inherent "otherworldly" reference... more like fantasy than anything else... precisely because what they are trying to show us in language drawn from this world is that our expectations of the new creation must not be constrained by our experience of this world.'[5]

There is an important point about plausibility here. *Prima facie*, the more plausible statement of hope for eternity might be to express it in very recognizable terms of this world. At least this would be easier to imagine. But in fact it fails to be plausible or even desirable – just because what we know now is all too evidently transient, decaying, and therefore actually unimaginable as eternity. In other words, more of the same does not convince! That is why we should not hesitate to let the full range and riot of biblical imagery be brought to bear, not just its safer images of continuity. This was a lesson well learnt and practised by early mystics and apophatic theologians. They either said nothing or everything, unleashing a torrent of images, each one taking the others further – and thereby pressing us to imagine a truly transcendent and perfected creativity, justice and love rather than just some fine-tuning of what we already know.

My first plea, therefore, is to make sure we develop basic biblical resurrection imagery from the wider resources within the biblical traditions themselves. The second plea now follows. In the light of this licence – and imperative – to conceive the truly transcendent, we should not too hastily abandon that apparently discredited Greek tradition. It may be worth mining further – not to rehabilitate it uncritically, but at least to take more seriously points where it can push us to think and imagine further.

Not surprisingly this means it must first be properly understood – and that leads us to realize that it is not always so polarised from the Hebrew tradition after all. For example, consider more carefully its language of soul. In fact it is not just conveying a conception of self with the soul as wholly separate, trying to escape a dispensable body. Admittedly, Greek thought certainly expressed discontent with aspects of our present bodily state (who in their right mind doesn't?). But that did not necessarily mean that one part of ourselves (the soul) must simply cast off another part of ourselves (the body) as though it were worthless. For Plato, 'soul' was far more complex and nuanced. It is the essence of all we are – and in that sense all that is most important about mind *and body* is actually part of 'soul'.[6] True, the present material nature of our bodies is not thought of as a permanent part of us, and does not survive death, but what we experience through our material bodies may still be taken by the soul into eternity. This could include all our relationships to people and the world, and even everything experienced through the body's material, sensual nature – anything from our experience of touch and laughter, to the scents of an English spring and the sights of an African sunset. In principle, all that is good from this material creation is potentially part of soul and part of eternity. In other words, the best of what matter and bodily senses has brought us in this world may be taken into eternity, even if not present matter itself. This good outcome of bodily life will be, in other words, 'kept as an inheritance for us in heaven' (to co-opt a biblical phrase). We could go further. Perhaps it is precisely this bodily life which has provided the potential for a unique texture and joy to heaven which could not have existed without this material world first having existed in this form? To be sure, this is now going beyond Plato himself, but it is nonetheless his language of soul which helps take us in that direction. In short – if we see past the caricature of Greek thought, its language of soul can actually help interpret the biblical vision, not contaminate it.

Is any of this conceivable? I believe it is. Even from within our bodily experience now we can sometimes sense that the contents of our consciousness – memory, will, feelings – may have more reality than our present, decaying bodies, and may even exist independently of them in some other way. This is not just conceivable for a few who have some out-of-the-body experience on an operating table (which I will say more about in the next chapter); it is also more widely acknowledged as conceivable in our quite ordinary instincts and language. After all, we quite naturally think of ourselves as being more than our present material bodies. That is why we instinctively talk about

Life Beyond Death

'having' a body rather than just 'being' a body. It is important to stress again that I am not wanting to abandon all body language for eternity, nor am I suggesting that our instincts simply express stark dualism of soul and body. Some sort of new embodiment may well be vital. In particular, it may be needed to express the sense that we will remain distinguishable, identifiable people, rather than being merged into some new cosmic whole. In that sense I do believe in the resurrection of 'the body'. However, that does not mean resurrection of the present material nature of our bodies. That has no more claim on eternity than matter in general in its present form – which, as modern physics tells us, is anyway ultimately more like a form of energy than a solid substance.

The main point remains, therefore, that we readily conceive ourselves to be more than our present bodies, and the mysteries of soul language are needed to express this. These may be more elusive than earthier images – but by the same token they may actually be more credible as we try to imagine eternity. They may even be more attractive as well. After all, we might be quite pleased with a divine love that did not just perpetuate the material nature of our present bodies!

Greek views of time and eternity are similarly worth revisiting. For again, if properly understood, they can push our thoughts in a useful direction. Admittedly, concepts of eternity are problematic when taken to exclude all sense of time and change. If they mean just static completeness, closing down creativity, denying any possibility of personal life, they offer little help. On that view we can understand Wright's insistence that we are safer thinking of life beyond death as a continuing story on a new earth rather than an eternal heaven. But again, that both underestimates the difficulty of staying just with those earthly time-bound images, and it risks ignoring the positive and more nuanced aspects of the Greek view which we may need after all.

For consider what it means if we only stay with images of time which are largely linear, always moving forward. Amongst other things, as we have seen, it will mean uncertain periods of 'waiting' after our death. And even after resurrection, it still implies an apparently infinite unfolding of more time and change. This itself carries its own implausibility – and at the very least it induces a certain sense of weariness. It is hard to express without conveying a sense of incompleteness and dissatisfaction: always travelling, never arriving. It leaves no possibility of meeting the theological demands for a *fulfilled* love and justice, the perfection of God's creation – those imperatives for an end to a groaning creation of 'death and mourning and crying and pain'. Such imperatives surely demand an end to the very structures of space and time which give rise to that pain and incompleteness. As such they require a state in which completion and fullness are suggested, not just creativity and change. They demand something much more like 'a house of God where there shall be no noise or silence, but one equal music, no fears nor hopes, but one equal possession, no foes nor friends, but one equal communion and identity, no ends nor beginnings, but one equal eternity'.[7] And what else is this but something very like the images generated by just that Greek-influenced tradition?

The critical point here is that such an image of an equal and complete eternity of 'no ends nor beginnings' can in fact be conceived dynamically. It does not have to mean complete timelessness, something static, undifferentiated, lifeless. Plato's eternity in the *Timaeus* may have done: but Plato's heaven *in toto* is not what I am arguing. I am wanting to take his instinct for perfection and completeness, and then marry it *to* creativity and dynamism.

But is that possible to imagine? Again, I believe it is. To do so we need first to characterize our *present* experience of time. As we know to our cost, this moves us inexorably from past through present to future in one direction. As such we never really inhabit it. We are always losing the past, however vividly remembered, and we are never actually *in* the future, however keenly we anticipate it. All we actually inhabit is the present but that too slips away into the past the moment we grasp it, which means that even the present is never quite real (philosophers call it a 'specious' present). So, in one way or another, time as we experience it is always slipping away from our grasp. Overall we currently experience a structure of movement and dynamism which is also inevitably a structure of loss, uncertainty, unreality.

This now sets the parameters of the positive task: can we imagine a way of transcending this in such a way that it retains the movement, but strains out the loss? I believe we can. The simplest way, to begin with, is by trying to conceive what we call past, present and future visually and spatially, as if it is laid out on a map. Think, for example, of a pattern of marks running across a piece of paper representing past, then present, then future. On the paper it is a two-dimensional linear sequence, one mark following the other. But because we do not just exist on paper, but in three dimensions, we do not have to follow the lines just in one direction. Our eyes can move in different directions, backwards and forwards, even up and down – so that we can inhabit it all as a whole and move around within the whole in an almost infinite number of ways. Now consider the relationship we have to the pattern on the paper to be at least a faint analogy of the relationship of heaven's eternity to earth's time. With its extra dimension, eternity can incorporate all the movement and changes of all our time without being bound just to one linear direction. It can always incorporate it as a whole, not losing any of it. (And it is interesting that some recent scientific cosmology is quite comfortable with something like this picture of time and space – which I will return to in the next chapter). Much the same could also be conceived through the analogy of music. Simply consider the experience of great music which is already known as a whole, but which can still be performed and heard in new ways, perhaps an almost infinite number of new ways. This is something we can do because, knowing it as a whole, we are already hearing the end from the beginning and can 'already' hear any one part afresh in the light of other parts. It is an experience of almost infinite depth and movement, yet within a perfect whole, and without loss.

Of course these are only faint and imperfect analogies, but

perhaps they help to see that it may be at least thinkable to posit this sort of eternity: i.e. an eternity in which the loss and unreality of linear time is transcended while retaining movement and life. This is a picture of an immensely satisfying eternity, which enables us to value both the completion of our travelling and the travelling itself. It is a picture opened up with the help of Greek images but which also helps meet those general theological imperatives which themselves require both the movement of love and its perfect fulfilment. It could also help unfold some more specific biblical images as well, and certainly need not contradict them. The Epistle to the Hebrews, for example, has images both of pilgrimage for the people of God, and a sabbath goal of rest and completion. It also has images of Christ's sacrifice which try to convey something happening both at *one* moment of time, but also reaching effectively backwards and forwards through *all* time. Whether or not there is specific Greek provenance to some of Hebrews' ideology and imagery is contested – but whatever its origin these images of the actual text can clearly play host to this sort of rich picture of eternity. It is also worth noting how this picture of eternity can help address those post-modern concerns mentioned briefly in the last chapter. That is, the anxiety about *endings*. Many contemporary novels and films struggle with endings – either they do not have clear endings, or they offer alternative endings. There seems to be a paralysis about completing a story for fear of killing it off, closing down options rather than keeping possibilities alive. This picture of eternity offers the dilemma a potential resolution. It offers the sort of eternity which is, precisely, an ending and completion which still includes endless possibilities within itself.

So – has all this provided a coherent answer to the questions of content and meaning by offering credible positive images of what heaven is actually like? Has it answered those most frequent specific, simple questions asked when people die: *where* is he? Will we see each other again? Will we have to *wait*?

Clearly it hasn't offered a simple answer. I still have to say that I do not really *know*, and what I believe I still cannot easily say. It certainly has not offered anything appropriate for those who are desperate and raw from immediate experience – no one in bereavement needs a discourse on theological method or Greek philosophy. But perhaps there has been at least something of answer in different terms. I hope there is enough here to help maintain general belief and shape hope, even if it is hardly appropriate for crisis moments. For what I have suggested does mean *something* determinate. It means we do not hope for heaven just as some extension or repetition of our present earthly life, simply with the flaws taken out. It means instead that we hope for a very new kind of experience where personal life and love and worship is still enjoyed, but enjoyed perfectly whole, with no decay of matter and no brokenness of time. And because of that, when we die we may not have to 'wait', for we may instantly enter with others this different kind of time in which there is no waiting (so that the biblical need to 'wait' is best seen just as a temporal metaphor for the non-temporal need to be truly complete). In the same way, when we rise we may not be restricted to any particular place, because, like the risen Christ, we shall not inhabit this sort of space and matter. Yet, at the same time, even within this radically different way of being, we may still hope to remain recognizably ourselves. We may even still be able to re-inhabit the best of our earthly experience as well: those footfalls of our memory, the rose garden, and children's laughter, fresh again, not fading. That is what it must mean to be in a perfect completed whole, with nothing lost.

Can this sort of hope be maintained truthfully, in the light of science and psychology? Can it be maintained morally so that we still live our lives now to the full? That is for the next chapter. As for this discussion on the *nature* of the hope, I will say no more, for I have almost certainly begun to say things whereof I should have been silent. But, if so, I can at least plead this excuse. Even if I have been tempted to hope for the wrong thing – but we cannot wait without *any* hope, and therefore cannot remain wholly silent.

Chapter 4

LIVING TRUTHFULLY WITH HOPE

If we look at the signs of transcendence around us we will find suggestions of heaven. If we also believe in a personal God of perfect creativity, profound love, and total justice, who is the God of Christ's resurrection, then we are driven to believe in heaven. We are bound to believe that there must be another kind of life for us beyond this one which is a perfect fulfilment of this whole creative impulse. If we are inspired by key biblical images, unfolded with the help of other conceptualities, we can even imagine a little what it might be like. It will be a radical act of re-creation: a reality which transcends and wholly re-configures the space and time and matter of our present existence .

But we do not believe this. Research into actual belief, within and beyond the church, suggests that it is not widely held. The findings of research mentioned in the first chapter suggested that less than half of churchgoers expressed any sure and certain hope of life beyond death in any form. There are many reasons for this unbelief, but amongst them is the one I now want to explore further: the recurring issue of *truth*. For the trouble is that it is all very easy to dismiss as mere wishful thinking.

This is an issue raised briefly before, but I now need to say more, because the very attempt to imagine such mysteries may have strained credibility rather than bolstered it. After all, what do we really mean by 'reorganized space, time and matter'? Does it connect at all with other ways of understanding reality, from science or philosophy? And if it doesn't, it becomes very vulnerable to the critiques of positivists from Durkheim to

Feuerbach and Marx, from Freud to A. J. Ayer and (until recently) Anthony Flew. Their questions have not gone away just because we're now in a generally more credulous postmodern age. In one way or another they keep asking: *are you really making any sense at all?* Above all: *how do you know you haven't just made this belief up?*

We will all have felt the force of this question in some way. We may know that we haven't consciously invented these beliefs ourselves, but that's not the main case of the sceptics. They are pointing to a more sophisticated mental process to account for the belief. They trace ways in which we may have made it up collectively and unconsciously, not just individually and consciously. We have done so, they say, out of some of our deepest needs and instincts: our need to bolster morality or social cohesion, our need to reassure ourselves in the face of the chaos outside in the world and inside ourselves; our need to compensate for the parents we have lost and the dreams which remain unfulfilled. Such things inevitably drive us to create an illusion of life beyond death. This sceptical viewpoint becomes even more compelling when much of the evidence in apparent support of our beliefs seems to come just from private and unverifiable experiences, or only in those ambivalent signs of experience we began with, or simply in that 2,000-year-old story of Christ we explored in the last two lectures. For even this story which may have convinced many in the past is now increasingly seen only as one story amongst others. So – what is the real cash value of this belief in the currency of *truth*, rather than mere wish fulfilment?

The screw is turned even harder when the currency being asked for is moral truth. It is not even as though we can cling to this belief because it is a self-evidently beneficial belief, a morally uplifting illusion. On the contrary, it is often held to be pernicious. Hope of afterlife, it is said, demotivates us for this life: it can prevent us from living life fully now, or trying to improve it now, for ourselves or others. For with hope in heaven hereafter why bother too much with here and now? Worse, as Marx suggested, it is a belief which can be pursued as a deliberate instrument of social control: people who have this hope for the future are more willing to accept hardship now – very useful for the privileged few who live off the backs of the hardship of the deprived majority. I briefly raised this issue too in the first chapter and promised to revisit it: it is another challenge to living truthfully with this belief.

What can be said in response to all this? Consider first the issue of wish fulfilment: the charge that we simply create the belief according to our needs. There is least one fallacy in this argument which can be disposed of immediately. It is an obvious flaw. The fallacy is to suppose that simply by identifying a social or psychological *origin* for a belief (especially if the origin lies in our needs), then its truth is undermined. This is not so. The mere fact I want or need something to be true, or the fact that society wants or needs something to be believed to be true, does not settle the question of its truth. The need and the wanting may well be a psychological or social mechanism by which the belief arises, but that has no necessary bearing on whether it is true or not.

Take a simple analogy. We may believe that our partner loves us, and has our best interests at heart. Someone then points out that because we badly want this to be the case we must be deluded by our wishes, and the love simply isn't there. That might in fact be the case, but equally it might not. There is no real *argument* here at all, only a suggestion prompted by associated ideas. It is no more an argument than suggesting that because we are hungry for food, food doesn't exist. In fact, if anything the reverse is more likely to be the case. Our deep hungers are sometimes a positive sign of the reality of that for which we hunger. It is a simple point, but it is often overlooked, and so the fallacy still needs to be unmasked when it is operating. It is called the 'genetic' fallacy: i.e. the view that because we identify a genesis or origin for a belief (especially an origin in our desires), this somehow discredits the content of the belief. It doesn't.

However, that is just ground-clearing. Is there anything more positive to support the truth of the belief? What happens, for instance, if we appeal to positive evidence of direct experience such as so-called near-death experiences?

Such experiences are often cited. One which has been especially influential is that of a ferocious sceptic, arch-positivist A. J. Ayer who consistently denied any possible meaning or truthfulness in such belief. That is, until June 1988, when he was 77 and his heart stopped for four minutes (apparently after choking on smoked salmon which had been smuggled in to his hospital bed by his former mistress!). He recovered – and then confessed the experience had completely changed his mind. He described having seen bright light and something like a river to cross.[1] This account forms part of a large body of well-documented evidence of so-called near-death and out-of-the body experiences which apparently show the persistence of consciousness after the body is clinically dead. These experiences are described in different ways using particular images according to people's previous belief systems, but most have some kind of family resemblance. For example, strong light often features (it can be found in accounts which range from a sixth-century middle-eastern holy man to a twentieth-century American worker trapped 'dead' under heavy machinery for 15 minutes).[2] Of these experiences A. J. Ayer's is often deemed one of the most convincing, precisely because he was an atheist. It was, after all, an experience against expectation, not projected out of his expectations. So all this has led to such experiences as these being subjected to serious interdisciplinary study.

Are they convincing? Even some of the most sympathetic enquirers are cautious. Theologian Carol Zaleski, for example, has written carefully and positively about them.[3] Yet even she finally takes them to be psychological phenomena which help reveal the deepest beliefs we actually hold, rather than compelling us to accept the truth of those beliefs. This seems to be clear from Ayer's experience, because he may not have been convinced after all. Apparently he reverted to his long held atheist belief once he had fully revived. In other words, it did not convince him in the end – and if it doesn't even convince the subject of the experience, its evidential value for the rest of us fades somewhat. It is a reminder that the very privacy of these experiences, their intrinsic subjectivity, is always their Achilles heel: they do not seem to provide good public evidence. (This is also true, it must be said, of many explicitly religious experiences including those of Christian mystics: many remain essentially private, publicly incommunicable, and therefore unverifiable).

On the other hand it could be said that they provide a different kind of public evidence – the transformed lives of those who have undergone them. Many do in fact testify to being changed (and there is a further, final, twist to the story of A. J. Ayer which could be used to support this in spite of his protestations that he remained sceptical: those closest to him testify that he was a changed person later in his life).[4] After all, a marked and lasting transformation of someone's life does generally provide a kind of public evidence to truth – especially if truth is deemed generally to be better revealed in a quality of life than in abstract argument or appeal to direct evidence: 'by their fruits you shall know them...' Some studies have therefore persisted in taking these experiences seriously as public evidence, tabulating clusters of them, demonstrating their family resemblances, and uncovering remarkable common features even where no collusion seems possible – of which the presence of light is just one. The early experiences of Christ's resurrection are sometimes audited in a similar way. They can be seen as multiple testimonies with real resemblances – and they certainly led to transformed lives. With this kind of public testimony, which philosophers call 'inter-subjective' evidence, perhaps we *can* therefore appeal to such experiences as positive, reasoned, empirical, evidence?

But I wonder whether this is really the only or best kind of path to tread in the search for truthfulness. Subjecting experiences to the methods of reasoned empirical enquiry and scientific method may play some part, but it is by no means secure as a method of enquiry. In particular it is not clear how we could ever really establish the truth of a belief about something which *transcends* this empirical world, simply by using the empirical tools *of* this world. It is like trying to capture the ripples of moving water by straining it out with a sieve. So when pressed for the truthfulness of the belief in terms of reasoned evidence, I would settle for something different. Rather than expecting compelling evidence, perhaps we should just look for some signs that there are at least *connections* with other forms of enquiry. We should look for knowledge from elsewhere (including the natural sciences) which at least helps show how the belief is imaginable, conceivable. It is a way of approaching truthfulness which completes the range of approaches taken in this book as a whole. Initially I was looking for a general context for belief in the signs of ordinary experience. Then I appealed directly to faith and we explicitly entered the Judaeo-Christian faith tradition to explore that. Now I am suggesting we draw these beliefs alongside other knowledge, simply to see if there are any points of imaginative connection.

This approach was signalled briefly in the last chapter, with the reminder from modern physics that matter is now seen to be less solid, more like energy, and so able to assume new forms. Writers like John Polkinghorne, the distinguished mathematical physicist, can now take us even further.[5] He also takes us into the imaginative connections set up by the new world of computers. He asks us to imagine that you and I resemble a computer software programme, a dynamic pattern of information, with our bodies representing the hardware of a computer system through which we operate. Conceiving ourselves like this we can see ourselves having a responsive, interactive, yet also enduring, identity – which, crucially, can also be operated through different hardware systems. It is an image of how our identity can be reformed and replayed through different systems after the decay of our particular current system, i.e. after our bodily death. Moreover, if there is any period of time elapsing between systems, our unique programme can still be held secure in the mind of the maker. There are problems with pressing this image too far, but at least it serves to indicate some points of conceptual and imaginative connection between what we need to think lies beyond our experience and other forms of knowledge which already lie within our experience.

Or consider another example: belief in a 'new heaven and earth'. As I have argued, this has to be conceived as a new environment we shall inhabit which we may call a new 'earth', but which – to be plausible – must radically transcend our current configuration of finite space, linear time and matter. Could this too be made thinkable with images drawn from other kinds of knowledge and discourse? Again, according to Polkinghorne, it is not wholly impossible. Mathematical physicists can 'readily think' that space-time-matter is not just as we currently experience it. Instead it can already be conceived as a sort of whole within which time is not linear as we now experience it, and matter is not bound to particular points of space and time as it is now (because matter is ultimately more like energy than solid particles). In short, it is a picture of reality not far from the sort of image of eternity we were looking for in the previous chapter: a state which combines completeness and dynamism. This picture of a new universe configured in this way would also allow it to coexist already with our present material universe, as a different dimension alongside it but capable of being accessed at any time. It may all seem far-fetched, even to motivated Christian believers, but it is actually a live subject amongst physicists. Even when unprovoked by theologians, they readily talk of conscious life being 'downloaded' out of space and time into a 'parallel' universe of such a different kind.

Assuming this *is* plausible, it is certainly an image which connects well with the theologian's concerns. It allows us to think of God holding both dimensions (the eternal and the temporal) within His overall plan and purpose. In other words, it helps us think of the new heaven and earth already held alongside this first creation – so that there is a continual process of redemption and resurrection as the dying parts of our creation are projected and transformed into this other dimension. Drawing on the previous image from computer software, it helps us imagine how all the best aspects of the information patterns of this world – persons, communities, even birds, animals and everything from the mountains to the music of its stars – are being constantly strained out of the old decaying order into the new: 'an inheritance kept in heaven for us. . .'

We should drop these pictures of information patterns, software, and further dimensions, if they are unhelpful or seem just bizarre. The point is not to press any particular analogy, but simply to show that the sorts of things we are impelled to believe by our theology about the other world are not wholly unconnected with images and discourses which have arisen within our known world – whether from IT or mathematics. And isn't this just what we should expect? As I have insisted before, there are good theological reasons why the other world should have some resonances with the reality of this world. That is how and why the meaning and truthfulness of what faith and theology impels us to believe, however difficult, can still be maintained. That is how and why we may say 'there are more things in heaven and earth than are dreamed of in your philosophy, Horatio' without needing to appeal to a mystery beyond *all* thought and imagining. For we are not silencing the quest for truth by an appeal to totally unconnected transcendence. We are suggesting instead that it is worth looking for other imaginings and philosophies to connect with – and we are sometimes finding them.

However, theological truthfulness isn't just a matter of what we can conceive or imagine – it is also about how we live. There is always an ethical dimension to truth to consider, as well as a conceptual or imaginative one. So we must also deal with that moral charge, for the hope to be believable: i.e. the charge that it undermines living responsibly and abundantly here and now.

In fact this is actually an important theological charge as well. It is a theological imperative to believe in life *before* death (as the *Christian Aid* slogan puts it), as well as life after death. Anything which undermines the quality of life now is as much a theological weakness as a moral one. This cannot be stressed enough. The biblical affirmation of this present life is massive. Even in the New Testament, where hope of afterlife is strong, we find the significance of this life emphasized just as much. Consider for example the Johannine emphasis on eternal life 'now', or the concern of the Synoptic Gospels with the Kingdom of God in the present. And even when the focus of the Gospels is on the resurrection narratives when one might expect an otherworldly emphasis, what is striking (and what distinguishes them from comparable accounts in the Graeco-Roman world) is actually their *reticence* about the next world. The risen Christ of these narratives tells us little or nothing about the world to come which he briefly entered and from which he returned. Instead, his emphasis is on comforting the disciples, and commissioning them for service in this world.[6] It all means that for any commitment to life after death to be both morally and theologically credible, it cannot possibly weaken this other emphasis on life before death. Indeed it must positively support it. So Karl Marx's charge doesn't just need to be refuted but turned on its head: we need to show that belief in life beyond death, far from weakening commitment to this life, positively enhances it.

How can this be done? First it is important to understand the full force of the charge *as it has been experienced*. We need for example to hear the powerful expression of feeling captured in this sort of summary statement: 'religion in general and especially belief in life beyond death has become a cosmic aspirin, an analgesic deliberately administered by the rich and powerful to dull the pain of the worker's lot'.[7] Another example comes from a survey of Victorian beliefs where heaven had become romanticised, just a place of family reunion and reunited lovers 'more like a middle class suburb in the sky than the City of God. . .an individualistic and exclusive heaven'.[8] The rhetoric of these kinds of comments very clearly shows how easily the belief was opened up to such serious criticism. It makes us hear how some forms of belief in afterlife have actually functioned in experience, as a matter of historical record, however unpalatable.

But therein lies the rub. Only some forms of the belief have functioned in this way, not all, and it is precisely the rhetoric of these quotations which betrays that these are only the parodied forms. They are referring to ideas about heaven which are just projections of wish fulfilment. They portray a heaven which only offers simple continuity with this world, and especially with the self-indulgent pleasures of the privileged of this world. In short, this is a heaven very far from the eternity we have been trying to imagine, with no regard for the *dis*continuity and mystery which I have stressed is also so necessary. It is also a heaven with no regard for the theological purposes of eternity: namely, those imperatives of fulfilling justice, perfect communion, and love. It is a heaven, furthermore, which gives scant regard to those specific biblical images and parables of the Kingdom of Heaven which make that purpose clear: the feasts which welcome the poor and the outcast, which have to do with justice for all, not just individual wish fulfilment; pictures about living mutually together in a way which is not just an extension of our present exclusive loyalties and prejudices. It is a heaven which ignores the fact that these biblical pictures have an imagery which straddles the present as well as the future, so what they portray of future justice must also affect the character of the present – making the charge that they undermine present social priorities absurd. To be sure, the church's teaching of heaven has not always reflected this character and challenge which is intrinsic to its proper theology. Its actual teaching has often been warped by its own social context – and in that sense the charge remains. But the response to that is to provide a proper view of heaven, and to recover the theology which should always be driving the belief, rather than drop the notion altogether.

Yet although this goes some way to mitigating the moral charge against heaven, there still needs to be more. For what lies behind the charge is not just the way a good belief has been distorted in a particular social context. There is also the charge that there is something intrinsically life-denying, or morally paralysing, about *any* belief in heaven – just because it is a hope beyond this world and this life. Any such hope, even if it is a hope of justice, is flawed because it is always the hope of a future which we cannot fully realize. As such it is like the backwash of a tide on a beach, constantly washing away our efforts to build lives now. The mere fact of expecting something beyond our efforts of this life relativizes everything we do now. It will always remind us that this life is ultimately just temporary sandcastles, no more than the grass that withers and the flower that fades, and so not worth the effort. Eternity simply stops us trying. So it is better not to believe it at all. It is better to take the moral high ground with unbelief.

Fortunately, this too is a flawed argument. It fails to grasp something already touched on, but whose implications I now need to make clearer. It does not understand the proper relationship between present and future, time and eternity, history and heaven. For it is crucial to grasp that eternity is not just a next stage to history, something which will simply follow on and *replace* what has gone before. Eternity does not succeed this life as if it is just the next thing on in linear time. Instead it is a new kind of complete and perfect reality which is more like a different dimension already standing alongside every point of time now. In this eternity, although new things may happen, there is also a completion and perfection of everything that has already happened – including what happens in our time. In short, eternity takes into itself all good things from time and history, holds them in completion, and does not let them slip back again into the stream of lost time. As Barth has said, our inheritance in heaven is a transformation of this world, not just new things following it. And from this picture of eternity, the moral implications for this life are most certainly not compromised in any way. They flow clearly and positively. It means that everything we do and are and strive for, here and now, is potentially eternal. Everything now is touched with infinite possibilities, whatever it leads to in time. In other words, it is the reverse of the charge being made. Only if the tide of time is all there is, will all our efforts now get washed away – whereas with this backwash of eternity everything in time retains its value. A Cambridge resident and theologian who experienced the 1952 Fenland floods, puts it like this: *'It's like in the floods... A sandbag team had toiled all day and seemed to have succeeded. Then when the last sandbag was placed — the whole dam was swept away. Wasted labour? No! I don't think so. An eternal building block had still been laid in the City of God.'*

This sort of relationship between time and eternity manifestly reverses Marx's charge. It gives us more moral motivation for this life — not less. It is also important to stress that it is a view of time and eternity which is genuinely part of the theological tradition. It is well grounded in the structure of resurrection hope. After all, throughout biblical narrative and doctrine 'resurrection' is thought of as happening to *all* time and history, not just to the end of it. That is the meaning of a 'general' resurrection: all will be raised, wherever they lie on the linear pathway of time, not just those at the end of it; all human history, not just its end, has the potential to be taken up into the new heaven and new earth. That is why God is described as God of Abraham, Isaac and Jacob as well as God of Bill and Sally and ourselves, and those who follow us. It is why God is described as 'the Lord of the living and the dead'. It is why, in the healing of nations at the end of time, every tribe and tongue is represented. It means that nations, tribes and tongues whose impact in history may have long since vanished in the stream of time, will also be raised — precisely because their value is eternal too. They were not just expendable means to some evolutionary end which left them behind.

So it is clearly a biblically grounded vision. It is also a hope taken into some of the best traditions of Christian poetry. Consider for example Thomas Gray's celebrated *Elegy in a Country Churchyard*. It is an extraordinary piece of work, a pre-Romantic vision, not sentimental even in its apparently homely images, but spare and visionary. It portrays precisely this potential for eternal value in the stuff of this ordinary life — the value of unknown lives buried beneath the tombstones. In worldly terms they were 'small' people who left no measure in empirical history. Their lives followed no measurable progress to any known glory. They lie without any visible sign of their value and achievements, just like discarded sandbags in a failed project. But by placing them in a Christian graveyard, the poet has deliberately asked us to see this different vision. He wants us to see that they lie there for resurrection. So 'let not ambition mock their useful toil/ their homely joys, and destiny obscure/ nor grandeur hear with disdainful smile/ the short and simple annals of the poor'.[9] As C. S. Lewis later put it, we all carry 'an eternal weight of glory' – whether or not that weight was recognised here and now.

The vision cashes out in specific ethical imperatives, as well as the general motivation to value people. For example, in the light of this sort of eternity how can the weak and elderly be left to go to the wall just because they may no longer leave much mark in time? They carry eternal value as much as anyone else. In the light of this sort of eternity how could we ever give up the global search for peace, justice and care of the earth, just because we may not always see its fruits in time? Even the very effort of seeking it is already a mustard seed of eternity. It is a vision which also teaches us to value ourselves, as well as others. In the light of this sort of eternity we cannot possibly think of ourselves as having no worth, whatever state we are in, for it is you and I who carry this weight of glory, as well as others. Moreover, it does all this in practice, not just in theory. This is not just rhetoric about the effect that a proper hope of heaven should have in principle, without any evidence that it works like this in practice. One telling example can be drawn from a recent survey of the beliefs of women in a housing estate in the north-east of England, and the effect these beliefs actually had on them. The survey first describes some of their struggles to bring up families in difficult conditions, their work for better social facilities – and then summarizes thus: '[their] belief in life after death is not a mere tranquilliser, making the women content with daily deprivation in the hope that all will be made better after death. It has a far more positive effect than this. Knowing that they have an eternal destination after death and an eternal dimension to their self ... gives them a sense of self-worth [now] that provides a basis for action and a foundation for self-determination. Without this eternal dimension it would be all too easy for these women to look at themselves with the eyes of contemporary middle-class society and judge themselves and their families as failures. Life after death enables them to live this life with greater courage and confidence'.[10] This is clear evidence from *lived* experience of belief – and perhaps the best counter of all to Marx's charge.

Lived belief of this kind also engages well with another moral concern. It addresses the post-modern preoccupation about endings, which I have mentioned before and to which I return because it is so haunting. The concern is to avoid conclusions which tend to seal all that has already happened and limit its meaning. It is the fear that if the narrator closes down the story the characters cannot re-narrate their lives in any different perspective – which means they will never be able to find redemption of the past, as well as never having new possibilities for the future. The specific ethical issue which then arises is to avoid 'concluding' other people's lives by trying to fix their meaning for them – for instance, by insisting that they are only fit for certain roles, must only live in one place ('the rich man at his castle and the poor man at his gate', or the asylum seeker always sent away). Instead, we should always give space for others to develop. It is a moral concern which extends to ourselves as well: it means we should not limit or close down our own lives, but always look to open them up. It touches, therefore, on common experience – the nagging quest for some new space or time to re-narrate our lives, to do or see things differently and to tell a different story about ourselves (even just a new job or holiday might do it – we think!). At worst this may just be an urge for novelty or self-indulgence, but at best it is looking for redemption. Rather than writing off ourselves or others, it is looking to a new future which also helps 'redeem' what has already gone before, rather than dismiss it, and which also gives further courage for that future.

All these concerns are met precisely through a Christian view of eternity, in the way the women of the survey embodied it. It offers a completion which does not close things down but opens them up – including what has already gone before. Without such belief the quest for this sort of fulfilment is bound to be frustrated, for we only have the resources of our finite human selves and we merely chase our own tails. On our own we cannot live on for ever to explore new possibilities and we cannot narrate our lives indefinitely to redeem our own past. We may try, but eventually we die, powerless to make a future to give our past any lasting value. We become like T. S. Eliot's old man in *Gerontion* who sits dramatizing his life in a sentimental reverie, which is ultimately just a sad fantasy. But with God and the hope of heaven, it is quite different. Then there is a real possibility, and a real hope, which deals with past, present and future.

This brings us finally to hope itself: to the simple point that hope *per se* is an overwhelmingly positive moral disposition and motivation, and hope of eternity particularly so. In the end there can be no doubt about this. Hope generally has long featured highly in moral estimation. It ranked as one of the three great biblical gifts: faith, *hope*, and love. Classically it has been one of the key Christian virtues. More recently it has been championed again by such as Ernst Bloch in his philosophy of hope and theologian Jürgen Moltmann in his theology of hope. In one way or another it has long been seen that hope is an essential moral dynamic − just for life itself: '*Dum spiro, spero* − as long as I breathe I hope. . .the breath of my soul is hope'. So − will this not be even more the case for eternal hope? Hope for this world alone, after all, is always vulnerable to disappointment. Neither scripture nor history and experience lead us to expect steady, visible progress towards the Kingdom in this world alone; we shall always live a roller-coaster of advance and retreat in moral and social progress. But hope which also reaches beyond this world is not vulnerable to such disappointments. Its dynamic for life can endure.

Moreover, an eternal hope generates a particularly *satisfying* ethic of motivation, as well as such an enduring one. Hope for this life alone has to make moral compromises − for even if we eventually achieved a lastingly better future in this world, it could only be experienced by those at that particular time in which it

Life Beyond Death

was achieved. It would exclude those building blocks washed away in the process of getting there. It would mean most people are only ever means to an end they will never share, rather than being part of that end. This is hardly a morally satisfying situation. It can even encourage an ethic of crude utilitarianism which too easily justifies sacrificing people in the present for this supposed future good. In contrast, hope for a radically new heaven and earth, which can *include* all that has gone before, creates a different ethic. It means we are always working for a final end of everyone's fulfilment, not their final sacrifice. It helps guard against the headlong rush to get into the future using other people just as means (how can we do that when the ultimate future belongs to them too?). It is a hope which moves us forward, but in a way which always includes the present, rather than treading it under foot. We move forward, as George Steiner puts it, 'in the slipstream of the statements we make about tomorrow's morning' – but always taking care of who is with us on the way. All this is entailed in the texture and shape of a true Christian hope which includes otherworldly hope – and it is certainly a long way from the caricature of some of its critics.

The critics of this belief still matter. It is often they who best test and purify belief. They certainly helped galvanise this book, and no doubt they will also have more to say which needs to be heard. Yet even if I have not answered adequately all the difficulties they raise, I hope I have now said something useful to help keep hope alive. I hope to have shown it is possible to attend to ordinary human experience and see the rumours of angels in it; possible to scrutinize the theological tradition, and find the rumours shouted aloud; possible to press that tradition hard for its conceptual and imaginative possibilities and find them. I hope that I have said enough, therefore, to show that we need not lose our nerve about hope itself, which is so life giving, not life diminishing.

And if this is so, why should we deprive people of this hope by our silence? Why on earth should we be so silent about heaven – inside and outside the church?

Towards the later part of his life, Michael Ramsey articulated his own simple endorsement to this need to speak of heaven, and the reason for it. When asked to compile a final anthology of his works, his editor asked what he would most like included. Later, the editor described what happened. There was a moment's silence, then Ramsey simply replied: 'Tell them about heaven! That's where we are going; that is what we were created for. Heaven is the meaning of our life here. Tell them about heaven.' And as he spoke 'there was a light in his eyes and an expression of glory on his face'.[11]

QUESTIONS AND ANSWERS:
CONTINUING THE CONVERSATION

What has been said in these four short chapters forms a kind of whole. It represents, I trust, a coherent approach to the question of life beyond death even though it is compressed within such a short space. But of course it is not anything like a systematic theology of life beyond death, even in outline. For instance, the major issues of traditional eschatology (parousia, judgement, hell, universalism) are hardly dealt with at all. Another area which could be developed is the christological centre of Christian belief about life beyond death. I have discussed the pivotal drama of Jesus Christ as a central event in the history of belief (chapter 2), and explored some of its distinctive meaning for life beyond death (chapter 3). But its significance as a uniquely *constitutive* event (as distinct from just a revelatory event) deserves much more than I have been able to provide here. This requires more consideration of the meaning of incarnation, not just the event of resurrection. For in much traditional theology the full meaning of incarnation is intrinsically soteriological – in the sense that opens the gate to eternal life just by its *happening*. We are saved and transformed, for this life and the next, by virtue of the very fact of the incarnation. This is especially true in the eastern tradition where the incarnation of God in Christ is the ground of our 'deification' and the sanctification of the whole material world. It draws humanity into God and God into humanity, earth to heaven and heaven to earth. The multi-layered meanings to this are then worked out in further doctrines, including the doctrines of atonement, creation, the work of the Holy Spirit, and ecclesiology. All this is rich systematic theological territory to explore which I have not pursued in this book.[1]

However, it is notable that all this traditional theological territory was *not* much pursued either by the audience at the original lectures on which this book is based. Almost no questions bore directly on incarnation, and very few asked about those other neglected areas of traditional eschatology of judgement and hell. It seems that the traditional canon of the theological agenda was not necessarily in people's minds! Instead, many remained focused on meta questions of truth, credibility and meaning, wanting more debate at this level.

This is surely important. It is vital to note what people actually wish to say and ask, rather than assume the further agenda for them. It is the only way to engage in real conversation, in theological matters as in others. In fact such a process is implicitly at work in most theology anyway to some extent, even without a further conversation. Thus the original text of these lectures was already a response to other people's questions beforehand, and the canon of theology on which they drew is already an accumulation and distillation of previous generations of theological questions and reflection. But because this is not always apparent, I have now added this record of the further specific questions and answers that the lectures provoked at the time. Quite apart from the intrinsic interest – and merit – of the questions themselves I hope it will also serve this other purpose: as a useful reminder that all talk and thought about God is a continuing conversation, in which we must be careful not to prejudge either the answers or the questions! To be sure, these are only the limited set of questions generated by particular audiences in a particular context. They will represent only one set of reactions and just one way of continuing a conversation. But they deserve attention nonetheless.

Both questions and answers are reproduced close to verbatim, but I have edited them a little to help clarity, and added a few extra comments in some answers to help refer to material elsewhere in the lectures. They are also grouped by subject matter, and not in their original order.

1. Questions about whether we can know anything transcendent, or anything beyond our own senses

Q. *Some time ago we were all mentally clobbered by extreme empiricism: the view that unless we could verify things by the senses it was nonsense. It was a kind of scientific reductionism. Scepticism about life after death, or lack of interest in it, is surely one of the inheritances of all this. Even if this kind of extreme empiricism is now less fashionable and decaying, do we not still need to confront these challenges of scientific reductionism?*

A. This sort of positivism, which was the extreme form of the philosophical challenge you are referring to, began earlier in the twentieth century and ran right through to the 1950s and 60s as a very influential movement – with particular influence here in the Anglo-Saxon world, even more than on the continent of Europe. It has now lost its force, as you imply. In its extreme form it shot itself in the foot by not even being self-consistent (it cannot even support its own premises, since it is not itself ver-ifiable by the senses!). It has also fallen foul of more general scepticism about the process of scientific reasoning. Nonetheless, I agree it is still alive and kicking in some form, and lies behind the work of e.g. Richard Dawkins and Peter Atkins. It is indeed a form of reductionism, or 'nothing-buttery' i.e. the view that the universe is *nothing but* what we can measure or hypothesize from empirical data. So the view develops that the universe is nothing but a blind evolutionary process arising out of chance and chaos, and with no ordering mind or force behind it; or that mind and consciousness is nothing but electrical impulses firing in the brain, so that the meaning of consciousness can be reduced to that description without remainder ... and so on. This is still influential to some extent.

Although this view may seem threatening, there is a sense in which I am glad to take it seriously – in fact more seriously as a theologian than many contemporary philosophers who are ready to dismiss it as outmoded. For in fact some contemporary phi-losophers and commentators easily reject this empirical-rational,

---

reductionist account in favour of a much more fluid, open-ended view of reality. Instead of attempting to talk of the 'real nature' or 'basic explanation' of things which can be found by attempting a rational or mechanical description, they prefer to tell stories to open up the many meanings which we create for things. This is very different from the hard-edged, rigorous, empirical reasoning of the positivists. However – I find it is these latter philosophers who at least have a sense of *truth* when they search for meaning: i.e. they have a sense that truth is, in principle, to do with *finding* meaning, rather than just an endless, playful, *creation* of meaning. They at least hold us to the view that when we encounter truth we meet something beyond us, as well as within us – whether we like it or not, whether it is the truth of God, or of no God, or a very 'reduced' truth of God. So I think we need them to keep holding us to that robust sense that we may sometimes encounter truth and have to accept it, rather than just create it as we like. In other words they hold us to a kind of realism – a view that some reality is there to be discovered, however partially, rather than just invented.

But why do I say this is not always threatening to religious belief, particularly in the form of some current scientific thinking? What is being discovered within this 'realist' assumption (especially by physicists) is sometimes quite hospitable to religious beliefs. For instance, as mentioned briefly in the lectures, they seem to find a universe in which matter may be more like energy (and mind may be bound up within it); they seem to find an open-textured universe suggestive of more possibilities than hitherto imagined. In short, the broad method and assumptions of realist empirical enquiry (though not its extreme form of logical positivism) can lead to an exciting and positive quest, not necessarily a reductionist one.

Interestingly, one of the authors of the original hard school of positivism, Anthony Flew, has recently changed his mind about God. I don't know why ... but he has!

Q. *Shouldn't we take more seriously the so-called spiritual revolution with its 'turn inwards' to subjective experience? Subjective experience matters most to people and isn't this is what is real?*

A. I agree we should take very seriously what lies 'within' and what we encounter in our subjective experience, but it is also important that this does not drain all sense of transcendence as well. In other words, to take seriously what is within need not be reductionist. In fact, the turn inwards is at best not a turn but a recovery of the essential fact that the God whom we find within ourselves, if it is really *God,* is also the God beyond ourselves as well. If the turn inwards does not find God within to be also God beyond, then I suspect we have lost the very meaning of God – we have only encountered ourselves.

2. Questions about maturity and whether we can face real endings

Q. *I like your image of the mother reassuring her child and expressing a sense of an ultimate good order which will continue, and I accept that. But there comes a time when the child recognizes that mother will die, which is quite normal. By then the child has developed its own capacity to hope – which has come through the mother, who represented this sense that good order and life will continue. I wonder if this means that the specific hope and belief in life after death is nothing more than an early primitive phase in the more mature idea of being able to sustain hope more generally for oneself?*

A. I think that the idea of growing into maturity in our beliefs, which you are pointing to, lies behind much of the psychological and social analysis of belief. This is why it was important to emphasize that death and the fear of death is not the only possible origin for religious belief and hope. For the same reason I have needed to argue that describing a social origin or context for a belief cannot itself determine the truth or otherwise of the belief [see chapter 4]. But I agree that your account for the origin of the belief is still a plausible one, even if not compelling.

Yet I am not so sure about your appeal to maturity. This begs some questions about what maturity means. Does maturity mean sheer independence? Does it mean being able to stand alone against what threatens us? I prefer to see maturity as seeking help from others to face in a creative way what threatens us, perhaps even to help us go beyond it. So maturity is not necessarily relying on our own resources. Nor is it necessarily looking clear-eyed at something threatening and saying 'I'm simply going to live heroically, facing it as it is'. Instead, true maturity might be looking at 'what is', with the help of others, in order to live with it and through it in a different way. In short, maturity might mean new kinds of dependencies, rather than the quest to rid ourselves of all dependence. The phrase 'man and woman come of age' is sometimes taken to mean that we live without dependency on God, and without the solace of false hopes and comforts of religion, but I'm not so sure that this is the sort of coming of age which brings real maturity. I see it as the state where we have come to accept that that we *do* need to depend on God and others, but we choose to do so in order to live more creatively and positively.

Q. *Rather than trying to commend the existence of life after death to those who are sceptical, wouldn't it be better to give a different kind of help, teaching, and guidance to them (and to clergy who advise them)? That is, shouldn't we now be helping people make use of eternity-type language in a non-supernatural way? So, for example, we can go on talking about infinity as mathematicians do, and recognize there are things beyond us, but we do not necessarily need to go into realms beyond this life. One reason why I pursue this is because we need to face endings. As Cupitt and others have said, the person who can never face endings can never finish anything. The person who cannot face up to his life coming to an end is encouraged by the church through the centuries to look to things beyond – but in doing that we do not live this life properly just because we do not live as though it is going to end.*

A. In fact the need to face endings is still vital even within a relatively orthodox view of afterlife. Resurrection is new life after a real and radical ending of death – it is not a seamless continuity [see Chapter 3]. So we are still faced with coming to terms with this ending and living our lives accordingly. And in any case, death as a final ending is not the only reason for living our life fully now. The prospect of this life being taken into eternity can also intensify the way we live now [see Chapter 4].

I think the underlying and deeper point you make is that you want to re-cast religious language and concepts in a non-supernatural way. Does this mean you want to reconceive God – and eternal life – to be wholly within the bounds of this life? I agree this may be what some people *want* to be helped to do, but it does not then follow that is what we *must* help them do. One thing is clear: if we do go down that path, we are no longer dealing with theology and the meaning of *theos* ('God'). We might still be using religious language, but it will be a very different religion.

Q. *David Hare, when researching for his play* Racing Demon, *describes how he found a fatal tendency of clergy to have one eye on this life and one eye on the next. Surely the best Christians are those who work as if there is no tomorrow... Isn't there a subtle loss of urgency amongst those who believe in the next life?*

A. If it is the case that most clergy have one eye on this life and one on the next, and this leads to a loss of urgency, then he is right to be concerned, but I wonder if that's true? If we look at the evidence, in a recent survey, of what is actually said by clergy on public occasions then in fact there is a focus on this life only. They appear to be reacting to what is happening here and now, and there is a remarkable *lack* of reference to the next life. This may not be all that is said, thought, or taught by clergy, nor is it necessarily a measure of their own deepest attitudes, but it is a guide. But however we read this evidence, the chief point I want to make again is that a *proper* focus on afterlife in fact intensifies our concern for this life, rather than diminishes it [see chapter 4]. There are many witnesses to this being the case, right the way through from biblical witnesses to those unnamed women of the north-east housing estate whose experience formed the basis of another survey.

3. Questions about our future bodies, creation, and the nature of heaven

Q. *If you think of 1 Corinthians 15 where St Paul is speaking both of the resurrection of the body and of immortality, is he being true to his Pharisaical tradition and just using 'immortality' to appeal to his audience, or is he perhaps beginning to do some of the work you have hinted at and heading in another direction [i.e. bringing more Greek - influenced notions of immortality to bear on Hebrew hopes for resurrection of the body]?*

A. I hope that Paul was heading in this direction, but I'm not sure he was! The Greek word he uses for spiritual body, for example, is *pneuma*, rather than *psyche,* and only if he had used the latter would I have been more confident that he was going down this path. So I tend to agree with Tom Wright's view that Paul is still thinking of the body (even the 'spiritual body' which is raised to immortality) as having some ultimate physicality about it. Yes, a different kind of physicality, but not yet reaching the point of such radically transformed matter that it is better described as a form of energy.

Yet some parts of the New Testament, and Paul himself, do perhaps move *some* way in this direction. Whenever they take on board notions of an intermediate state without embodiment, there are at least the stirrings of a possibility that the new embodiment we shall finally have should be more 'spiritually' described, and less materially bound. So *perhaps* here in I Corinthians, as in other places, Paul is being impelled to hint at more than he may have actually believed at the time!

Q. *Jesus would obviously be familiar with the debate between the Sadducees and the Pharisees over the resurrection and he consistently talked about the Kingdom of Heaven. Do you think he was hinting at a re-created perfect heaven on earth or a perfect heaven elsewhere, and if so how would it be?*

A. 'Thy Kingdom come on earth, as it is in heaven', is the phrase which most obviously springs to mind. Clearly his hopes *included* hopes for this world, but is that all? It is perilous to try to reconstruct the historical Jesus' exact beliefs and expectations, and I can't be sure. In fact I would expect him to have been largely 'earthbound' in his conception, in the sense that he would look to this world being transformed, in line with many current Jewish beliefs. But I doubt it was just that. At times it seems that he envisaged a very radical transformation at 'end times'. What's more, a good deal of his parables about the Kingdom of Heaven see it already here in some sense, but also look to a quite different sort of fulfilment in the future where its final reality is of quite a different order (for example, the parable of the seed and the mustard tree).

I am fascinated by the theme of growth in many of these parables of the Kingdom, and the more I look at them the more I think this is not about some uniform linear growth like progress. Instead, the picture is of God making something quite new emerge – which may well include 'heaven elsewhere'. In general, though, the difficulty is that we easily project on to Jesus what we find elsewhere in the New Testament, and our own beliefs, just as the evangelists themselves were doing. So I find the historical Jesus' own exact sense of things hard to disentangle.

That doesn't mean it fails to give us guidance. The cumulative understanding which we gain, especially from the New Testament as a whole, and our continued reflections on it, does lead us to real hopes and beliefs. These have led me to think that there is a reality truly beyond this world, which fulfils the best of this life, but also goes beyond it. So that is why I have argued that the Kingdom of Heaven is *both* on earth, *and* beyond.

Q. *You talked generally about all creation – but what may we believe of the animal creation? Having found a decapitated little bird I found myself driving to a beautiful spot to bury it. Is this just sentiment?*

A. Once we think of this whole creation as the desired work of a creator God who 'looked at what He made and saw that it was good', then the possibilities that any of it is just doomed to extinction seem remote! The notion that the only final outcome will be a few chosen human souls extracted by God from their embodiment and allowed to exist in the ether does not make sense. It seems much more likely that what we have experienced through our bodily senses, including the animal world, the mountains and rivers, sea and sky, will indeed find some sort of reality in a new heaven and new earth. Although this may sometimes sound incredible, there are ways of imaging and conceiving this [see chapters 3 & 4], and many good reasons to think it might be so.

Q. *This is a question from the coal-face of funeral visits. So many people today are convinced, and wish to tell me, that their beloved who has died is now with the rest of the family. They are not going to budge from that belief – and I feel cowardly that I cave in to it and kick myself afterwards because somehow I want to enlarge their feeling of what is beyond – in a Christian way – but I don't know how to bridge the gap with their expectations.*

A. In fact I do not find myself wanting to disabuse people of this sort of notion. Of course, the way that people talk about it may seem sentimental or naïve, but isn't so-called naivety sometimes the tip of an iceberg of reality? If anything, what I have said about the possibilities of transcending our current experience of time [see chapter 4] suggests that someone who has died may indeed be 'already' with others who have died before – at least in their experience. As I have also said, I certainly believe that we may hope to recognize others beyond this life as distinct, unique people, however greatly we are all changed. As Teilhard de

Chardin has said, *love* always wants to enhance uniqueness, not to suppress it, so will not this also be true in heaven? So – I don't feel the need to take away the comfort of this sort of belief.

To be sure, it will be different. There was some fascinating work done recently by psychologists who looked at the state of that part of the brain which distinguishes between the self and others when we are in deep meditation, or when we are in a state of great exaltation like being in love. At such times, curiously, that part of the brain which distinguishes between the self and others is almost dormant, as though the boundaries are blurred. This may give a hint of the difference. The relationship between self and others is still there, but perhaps in perfect love we are so much more one with others that we lose the boundaries and exclusiveness of some our relationships. 'There is no marriage or giving in marriage in heaven' is perhaps a warning against translating into heaven the (proper) exclusiveness and limits of some of our current relationships in this life. Yet there is still *relationship* in heaven, even if a different kind.

This may seem a strange way to answer your question, and not the sort of way we would talk at the raw time of grief and immediate bereavement. But I would still love us to be able to discuss these sorts of things, in these sorts of ways, as part of our *general* church teaching and conversation – as part of the background we bring to those moments of crisis when it's often inappropriate to say very much at all. Together, we need to explore new ways of imagining ourselves which transcend the way we are now, and that will be part of what we bring to our hopes for those who have died.

4. Questions about getting to heaven

Q. *I have some concerns about eternity as a sort of moral imperative. Isn't there the danger of believing that we earn heaven by our good works?*

A. I prefer to see the reality of heaven as a moral attraction, rather than a moral imperative. It is something to which we are drawn, rather than something by which we are pushed (though I think we can be pushed to *belief* in heaven by moral issues, such as the imperative of fulfilling love and justice). I understand heaven to be a state we would want to enjoy and inhabit, as the images of the Christian tradition convey. I certainly agree that it is only possible for any of us because of the grace of God, rather than our moral striving. Perhaps, too, it is only possible if we do actually *want* to be there. I also believe Jesus Christ has a central role in making this possible – though the nature of that role certainly deserves at least another set of lectures. [See p. 75.]

Q. *If, as you argue, there is life after death, do you conceive this as a life to which everyone has access? Does the argument from justice require that this is a life from which some are excluded? I'm wondering about the place of judgement in the scheme of things.*

A. I have focused on eternal *life* beyond death – not judgement or extinction – but this remains a fair and inescapable question. As I understand it, there is judgement for us all, in the sense of a necessary discernment. Interestingly, this necessity for discernment is also often referred to outside the explicitly religious or biblical frame. It sometimes features, for example, as a 'review of one's life', often associated with near-death experiences. It is also one of the motifs of the current concern with narrative. As I have mentioned, many of us feel the need to 're-narrate' our lives in some way. We actually want to see our lives, at times, in a different perspective, and we want the opportunity to do this. In that sense, we may all want and need 'judgement'.

Of course, this is not necessarily the same as the divine judgement whose discernment leads to executing retributive justice – of the kind that simply writes some people off. But does true discernment ever lead to this? In other words, would true discernment lead either to God simply deeming some of us to be irredeemably unfit, or lead some people to decide they did not *want* to live with God? I do not know, but I do know that retributive justice is by no means the only or best sort of justice –

and God's justice will surely be the best. In any case, there are strong strands within the biblical tradition which give hope that all will be able to live with God: 'as in Adam all die, so in Christ shall all be made alive...in Christ *all* things are reconciled'. This may only refer to all *kinds* of people and all kinds of things, but the logic of it may still be truly universal. In the end, I do not know, but we can trust that God's judgement will be just and will be seen to be just. And we can trust that God's justice is true justice which we will all recognize to be also a true expression of God's love.

5. A challenge for the church

Q. *The question I am left with is this. In long lectures, when you discuss and sometimes disabuse us of the traditional baggage of imagery, you can carefully gloss what you say. But I struggle with how one deals with this in an ordinary church context.*

A. I think we would all agree that the particular moments when these issues most obviously surface, especially at times surrounding death and bereavement, are often precisely *not* the times for extended discussion. However, I hope that churches are not just involved with people at these moments. We aim also to be involved in a long process of living and learning and teaching together. In some church life there is usually some opportunity for teaching and conversation in a way which is more than brief 'hit and run' mission! We are working with people as a community. That is when these sorts of issues can be discussed, disagreed about, revised, and 'made our own'. These are the contexts in which our thinking and talking about heaven can often best happen in a way which is neither crude, nor insensitive, allowing a full range of doubt and belief to be aired. (I realize churches cannot always achieve this sort of long-term community life, especially in today's fragmented culture, but we work at it!)

This means that we are not going to be able to introduce new images and creative ideas just by a single sermon, or by adding a few new words to a liturgy. It will take a more serious and open teaching and learning culture for church life as a whole. I have no doubt that many within our churches are longing for this. They want the opportunity for extended discussion about basic beliefs, and they are willing to take risks with questioning some received images. Of course there is always the fear of being misunderstood, either by giving false comfort with new images or by undermining cherished belief when traditional images are discarded. But if we do not take the risks and simply lapse into silence, we do not serve people well because they may be left just with discredited images and secret doubts, and that cannot adequately nourish hope.

I will end with an anecdote. Some time ago I found myself talking to someone whose life work had involved him in studying existentialist literature – a philosophy which insists that we create meaning for ourselves, and there is no meaning 'beyond' at all. When his wife died he simply said 'I thank God for Christianity, because at least it gave me hope'. Somehow, Christians of his church had created for him a community in which thoughtful hope had been articulated and kept alive, in many ways and at many levels. That's surely our aim.

NOTES

Introduction

1. See e.g. Paul Heelas and Linda Woodhead, *The Spiritual Revolution* (Blackwell, 2005) for some general trends in spirituality. The kind of theology which speaks of a non-personal God is often non realist, but may also appeal to older traditions of apophatic theology.
2. E.g. *The Guardian*, December 5 2005: review by Polly Toynbee of *The Chronicles of Narnia*.
3. I have discussed these in some depth in Vernon White, *Identity* (SCM, 2002).
4. Ibid.
5. I use the personal pronoun 'He' for God throughout, to retain a sense of the personal nature of God: but it should not be taken to mean that God is exclusively male.

Chapter 1: THE PERSISTENCE OF TRANSCENDENCE

1. Michael Ramsey, *Sacred and Secular: a study of the otherworldly and this worldly aspects of Christianity* (Longman, 1965).
2. Douglas Davies and Alistair Shaw, *Re-Using Old Graves; A Survey of Popular British Attitudes* (Shaw & Sons, 1995).
3. There is some interesting evidence, for example, in Ellen Clark-King, *Theology by Heart* (Epworth, 2004), ch 6.
4. Tony Walter, *The Eclipse of Eternity. A Sociology of the Afterlife* (Macmillan, 1996).
5. Bronislaw Malinowski, *Magic, Science & Religion* (1925): reprinted in Antonius Robben, *Death, Mourning, and Burial* (Blackwell, 2004).
6. One early study is Jeop Munnichs, *Old Age and Finitude* (Karger, 1966). I am indebted to Professor Peter Coleman for this and for comments from his research at Southampton University.
7. John Bowker, *The Meanings of Death* (Cambridge, 1991).
8. Peter Berger, *A Rumour of Angels* (Penguin, 1969).
9. C. S. Lewis, *The Weight of Glory* (1941).

10. Penelope Fitzgerald, *A House of Air* (Harper, 2005), p. 472.

11. George Steiner, *Real Presences* (University of Chicago, 1989).

12. John Polkinghorne, *The God of Hope and the End of the World* (SPCK, 2002).

13. Bowker, *The Meanings of Death*, pp. 215–16.

Chapter 2: THE CRISIS OF DEATH AND THE CREDIBILITY OF THEISM

1. Bertrand Russell, *Mysticism and Logic and Other Essays* (London, 1918).

2. Alan Segal, 'Life After Death: The Social Sources' in S. T. Davies *et al* (eds) *The Resurrection: an interdisciplinary symposium on the resurrection of Jesus* (Oxford, 1997).

3. Psalm 90.

4. Henry Scott-Holland, 'The King of Terrors', a sermon preached on 15 May 1910.

5. Psalm 73:26, 24.

6. N. T. Wright, *The Resurrection of the Son of God* (SPCK, 2004).

7. Isaiah 26:19.

8. Daniel 12:2.

9. Wright, *The Resurrection of the Son of God*.

10. A. J. M. Wedderburn, *Beyond Resurrection* (SCM, 1999).

11. 1 Corinthians 15:16, 20.

12. Romans 8:38.

13. cf Alan Wilkinson, *Dissent or Conform? War, Peace and the English Churches 1900–1945* (SCM, 1986).

14. cf Frances Young, *Face to Face: a narrative essay in the theology of suffering* (T. & T. Clark, 1990).

15. e.g. Rosemary Radford Ruether, *Gaia and God* (SCM, 1993).

16. e.g. Elizabeth Johnson, *Friends of God and Prophets: A Feminist Theological Reading of the Communion of Saints* (SCM, 1998).

17. Walter, *The Eclipse of Eternity*.

18. Joao Cabral de Melo Neto, 'The Death and Life of a Severino' taken from *Selected Poetry 1937–1990* (Wesleyan University Press, 1994).

19. Nicholas Wolterstorff, *Lament for a Son* (Eerdmans, 1987).

Chapter 3: MEANINGS OF RESURRECTION

1. T. S. Eliot, *Four Quartets* (Faber & Faber, 1943).

2. Anthony DeStefano, *A Travel Guide to Heaven* (Doubleday, 2003).

3. *Times* review, 2004.

4. John Donne, *Sermon* (1627).

5. Richard Bauckham and Trevor Hart, *Hope Against Hope* (DLT, 1999), p. 107.

6. Cf. an interesting discussion by Stephen Clark, *A Parliament of Souls* (Oxford, 1990), pp. 139–40.
7. Donne, *op.cit.*

Chapter 4: LIVING TRUTHFULLY WITH HOPE

1. This has been documented and widely discussed in a number of sources. See for example Douglas Shrader, 'Near-Death Experiences: Scientific, Philosophical, and Religious Perspectives', *Oneonta Philosophy Studies* (New York 1995): cf. www.oneonta.edu/academics/philos/NDE.html;
2. Cited in Kathleen Fischer, *Imaging Life After Death* (Paulist Press, 2004).
3. Carol Zaleski, *The Life of the World to Come: Near-Death Experience and Christian Hope* (Oxford, 1996).
4. Cited in an article by William Cash, *National Post*, 3 March 2001.
5. Polkinghorne, *The God of Hope and the End of the World.*
6. cf A. J. M. Wedderburn, *Beyond Resurrection.*
7. Bauckham and Hart, *Hope Against Hope*, p. 55.
8. Michael Wheeler, *Heaven, Hell and the Victorians* (Cambridge, 1990), p. 121.
9. Thomas Gray, *Elegy.*
10. Clark-King, *Theology by Heart*, p. 181.
11. Cited by Lorna Kendall (ed.), *Gateway to God: Daily Readings with Michael Ramsey* (DLT, 1988).

Postscript

1. I have touched on the constitutive nature of the Christ event in a previous book *Atonement and Incarnation* (Cambridge, 1991), and in a more recent essay: 'Varieties of Uniqueness and the Person of Christ' in T. W.Bartel (ed.), *Comparative Theology: essays for Keith Ward* (SPCK, 2003). These discuss meanings of incarnation more fully (though they do not specifically relate them to life beyond death).

INDEX OF NAMES

Marx, K. 58, 66, 69, 71
Moltmann, J. 72
Mozart, W. A. 42
Munnichs, J. 89n

Nietzsche, F. 17, 40

Owen, W. 34

Plato 28, 48, 52, 54
Polkinghorne, J. 19, 63–4, 89n, 91n

Rahner, K. 24
Ramsey, M. 8–10, 12, 38, 74, 89n
Reuther, R. R. 90n
Robben, A. 89n
Russell, B. 24–5, 39, 90n

Scott Holland, H. 8, 26, 90n
Segal, A. 25, 29, 90n
Shakespeare, W. 13
Shaw, A. 89n
Socrates 47

Steiner, G. 19, 22, 73, 90n

Toynbee, P. 89n
Traherne, T. 17

Vaughan, H. 48

Walter, A. 11, 89n, 90n
Wedderburn, A. J. M. 90n, 91n
Weil, S. 18, 24
Wheeler, M. 91n
White, V. 89n, 91n
Wilkinson, A. 90n
Wittgenstein, L. 4, 41
Wolterstorff, N. 90n
Woodhead, L. 89n
Wordsworth, W. 13, 17
Wright, N. T. 30, 43–4, 48, 53, 82, 90n

Young, F. 35, 90n

Zaleski, C. 61, 91n

Index of Names